OXFORD
UNIVERSITY PRESS

ASPIRE
SUCCEED
PROGRESS

Cambridge Lower Secondary

Complete

Chemistry

Philippa Gardom Hulme

Second Edition

WORKBOOK

Oxford excellence for Cambridge Lower Secondary

OXFORD

OXFORD
UNIVERSITY PRESS

Great Clarendon Street, Oxford, OX2 6DP, United Kingdom

Oxford University Press is a department of the University of Oxford. It furthers the University's objective of excellence in research, scholarship, and education by publishing worldwide. Oxford is a registered trade mark of Oxford University Press in the UK and in certain other countries

British Library Cataloguing in Publication Data
Data available

978-1-38-201860-9

10 9 8 7 6

Paper used in the production of this book is a natural, recyclable product made from wood grown in sustainable forests. The manufacturing process conforms to the environmental regulations of the country of origin.

Printed in China by Golden Cup

Acknowledgements
The publishers would like to thank the following for permissions to use copyright material:

Cover illustrations: Dario Bosi/Getty Images.

Artworks: QBS Learning, Integra

Every effort has been made to contact copyright holders of material reproduced in this book. Any omissions will be rectified in subsequent printings if notice is given to the publisher.

IGCSE® is the registered trademark of Cambridge Assessment International Education

This Student Workbook refers to the Cambridge Lower Secondary Science (0893) Syllabus published by Cambridge Assessment International Education.

This work has been developed independently from and is not endorsed by or otherwise connected with Cambridge Assessment International Education.

Introduction

Welcome to your **Cambridge Lower Secondary Complete Chemistry Workbook**.

This workbook accompanies the Student Book and includes one page of questions for every two pages of the Student Book. Each question page includes several types of question.

- Some questions ask you to choose words to complete sentences. These questions will help you to learn and remember key facts about the topic.

- Other questions ask you to identify statements as true or false, or put statements in the correct order. Some of these questions are testing your knowledge, others are asking you to apply what you know to a new situation.

- There are many questions that ask you to interpret data from investigations, or information from other sources. When you answer these questions, you will be practising important science skills, as well as preparing for the Cambridge Checkpoint test.

- Some pages include comprehension questions. They ask you to read some information, and then answer questions about it. Many of these questions will help you develop skills of evaluation.

- Most pages have an extension box. Some of these questions will help you to extend and develop your science skills. Many others go beyond Cambridge Lower Secondary Science. They include content equivalent to Cambridge IGCSE and O level. All the extension questions are designed to challenge you, and make you think hard. There aren't any spaces for your answers to these extension questions, so you'll need to work on a separate sheet of paper.

This workbook has other features to help you succeed in Cambridge Checkpoint and eventually Cambridge IGCSE:

- The glossary explains the meanings of important science words.

- The questions are excellent practice for the Cambridge Checkpoint test. They have been especially written by the author to provide lots of practice before your exam.

- Thinking and working scientifically, and Science in context questions are indicated in the margin using the symbols on the right.

- The Extension practice questions show you what you are aiming for. Give them a try!

I wish you every success in science, and hope you enjoy the workbook.

Contents

Stage 9

The periodic table of the elements

1	2	3	4	5	6	7	8	9	10	11	12	13	14	15	16	17	18
1.0 H hydrogen 1																	4 He helium 2
7 Li lithium 3	9 Be beryllium 4											11 B boron 5	12 C carbon 6	14 N nitrogen 7	16 O oxygen 8	19 F fluorine 9	20 Ne neon 10
23 Na sodium 11	24 Mg magnesium 12											27 Al aluminium 13	28 Si silicon 14	31 P phosphorus 15	32 S sulfur 16	35.5 Cl chlorine 17	40 Ar argon 18
39 K potassium 19	40 Ca calcium 20	45 Sc scandium 21	48 Ti titanium 22	51 V vanadium 23	52 Cr chromium 24	55 Mn manganese 25	56 Fe iron 26	59 Co cobalt 27	59 Ni nickel 28	63.5 Cu copper 29	65 Zn zinc 30	70 Ga gallium 31	73 Ge germanium 32	75 As arsenic 33	79 Se selenium 34	80 Br bromine 35	84 Kr krypton 36
85.5 Rb rubidium 37	88 Sr strontium 38	89 Y yttrium 39	91 Zr zirconium 40	93 Nb niobium 41	96 Mo molybdenum 42	(98) Tc technetium 43	101 Ru ruthenium 44	103 Rh rhodium 45	106 Pd palladium 46	108 Ag silver 47	112 Cd cadmium 48	115 In indium 49	119 Sn tin 50	122 Sb antimony 51	128 Te tellurium 52	127 I iodine 53	131 Xe xenon 54
133 Cs caesium 55	137 Ba barium 56	139 La lanthanum 57	178.5 Hf hafnium 72	181 Ta tantalum 73	184 W tungsten 74	186 Re rhenium 75	190 Os osmium 76	192 Ir iridium 77	195 Pt platinum 78	197 Au gold 79	201 Hg mercury 80	204 Tl thallium 81	207 Pb lead 82	209 Bi bismuth 83	210 Po polonium 84	(210) At astatine 85	222 Rn radon 86
(223) Fr francium 87	(226) Ra radium 88	(227) Ac actinium 89	(261) Rf rutherfordium 104	(262) Db dubnium 105	(266) Sg seaborgium 106	(264) Bh bohrium 107	(277) Hs hassium 108	(268) Mt meitnerium 109	(271) Ds Darmstadtium 110	(272) Rg roentgenium 111							

Note: This periodic table does not include all the elements.

1. Use words and phrases from the box to complete the sentences below.
   Use each word once, more than once, or not at all.

rock	particles	materials	sugar	silver	mixtures	substances

The different types of matter that things are made from are .... All materials are made

up of tiny .... Most materials are .... They have different types of particle.

Some materials are made up of one type of particle only. They are .... Examples of

substances are .... and ....

2. The particle model explains properties. Draw one line from each factor to the one difference in
   properties that it explains.

Factor
particle separation
particle mass
if and how the particles move
how strongly the particles hold together

Difference in properties that the factor explains
why a gold coin is heavier than a silver coin of the same mass
why liquid water flows but solid rock does not flow
why 1 g of ice takes up less space than 1 g of steam
why gold is easier to scratch than diamond

Extension

Write the letter of each phrase below in the correct part of the diagram.

a. Made up of particles

b. Made up of identical particles

c. Pure water, for example

d. Most types of rock, for example

e. Its properties describe what it is like and what it does

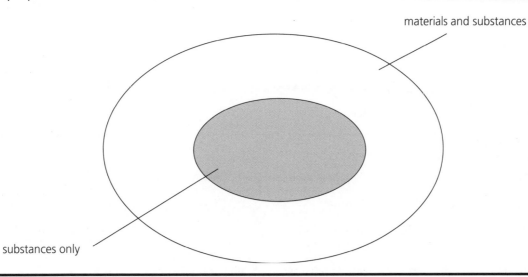

materials and substances

substances only

1. Highlight the correct **bold** words in the sentences below.

   There are **two / three / ten** states of matter. A substance can flow in the liquid and **solid / gas** states. You can compress a substance a lot in the **solid / liquid / gas** state. A substance takes the shape of the bottom of its container in the **solid / liquid / gas** state. A substance takes the shape of its whole container in the **solid / liquid / gas** state.

2. **a.** In the box, draw the arrangement of particles in a substance in its solid state.

   b. Describe the movement of the particles in the solid.

   ....

3. A student drew the diagram below to represent the particles in a liquid.

   Explain what is wrong with the diagram, and draw a better one in the empty box.

   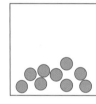 

   ....

4. Write the letter of each phrase below in the correct part of the diagram.

   A. Made up of particles

   B. Takes the shape of its whole container

   C. Particles move from place to place

   D. Particles touch each other

   E. Can be compressed only a tiny bit

   F. Particles are not in a pattern

   G. Flows

   H. Particles are in a regular pattern

   I. Particles do not move from place to place

   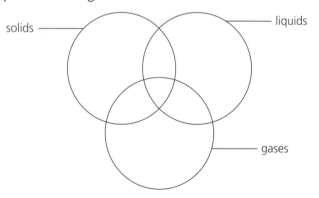

Extension

The statements below are about the particles in a liquid. They are all correct.

   P The particles hold together strongly.   **Q** The particles touch each other.

   R The particles move around, sliding over each other.   **S** The particles are not in a regular pattern.

a. Write the letter of the statement that best explains why you can pour a liquid. Explain your choice.

b. Write the letter of the statement that best explains why the volume of a liquid does not change when you pour it into a bigger container. Give reasons for your choice.

1. Write down one use for each of the substances below.

   a. Carbon dioxide ....

   b. Oxygen ....

   c. Water ....

2. Circle the letter next to the best definition of a vacuum in science.

   A. It is a device for cleaning floors.

   B. It is a space that has no matter in it.

   C. Outer space is a vacuum.

   D. It is a space that has very few particles in it.

3. Draw one line from each property to the factor that explains it.
   Two of the lines go to the same factor.

Property
A substance flows in the liquid and gas states.
A substance can be compressed only a tiny bit in the solid and liquid states.
The shape of a substance in the liquid or gas state depends on the container it is in.
A substance can be compressed a lot in the gas state.

Factor that explains it
The particles touch each other.
The particles move around.
The particles are in fixed positions.
The particles are far apart.

Extension

Suggest one observation or short experiment that provides evidence for each statement below.

a. In the gas state, particles move very quickly.

b. In the liquid state, particles move around randomly.

c. In the solid state, particles do not move around.

d. In the gas state, the particles are further apart than they are in the solid state.

1. Write **T** next to the statements that are true. Write **F** next to the statements that are false. Then write corrected versions of the **two** statements that are false.

   a. Condensing is the change of state from liquid to gas.

   b. When a substance condenses, its particles get closer together.

   c. When a substance changes state from liquid to gas, its particles get closer together.

   d. The more strongly the particles of a substance hold together, the higher its boiling point.

   Corrected versions of false statements:

   ....

   ....

2. Look at the diagrams.

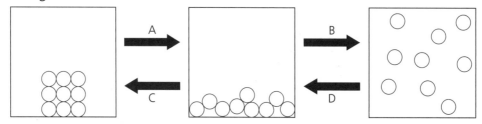

   a. Give the letter of the arrow that shows condensation. ....

   b. Give the letter of the arrow that shows boiling or evaporation. ....

3. For each statement, write a tick (✓) in the correct box in the table.

	True of evaporation only	True of boiling only	True of both evaporation and boiling
This involves a change of state from a substance in its liquid state.			
Particles leave the surface of the liquid only.			
Bubbles of the substance in its gas state form throughout the liquid.			
This can happen at any temperature.			
During this change of state, the particles get further apart.			

Extension

The table gives the boiling points of six substances.

Substance	Boiling point (°C)
ethane	−89
hexane	69
hexadecane	287
heptane	98
methane	−162

a. Name the substance in the table that has the lowest boiling point.

b. Name the substances in the table that are in the gas state at 20 °C.

c. Name the substance in the table whose particles hold together most strongly.

Thinking and working scientifically

1. Draw one line from each word to its definition.

Word	Definition
hypothesis	A piece of data that does not fit the pattern in a series of results.
anomalous result	A possible explanation that is based on evidence and that can be tested further.
conclusion	A description of what an experiment shows, with an explanation.

2. Yana measures the boiling point of pure water. She adds salt to the water. She measures the boiling point of the salty water. Her results are in the table.

Substance or solution	Boiling temperature (°C)
pure water	100
salty water	104

Yana makes a hypothesis based on the data in the table:
The more salt in the water, the higher its boiling point.

a. Suggest how Yana could test her hypothesis, using the apparatus in the list below:

- beaker
- thermometer
- Bunsen burner, tripod and gauze
- small spoon

....

....

....

b. Yana obtained the results in the table.

Number of spoonfuls of salt	Boiling temperature (°C)
0	100
1	102
2	104
3	101
4	108
5	110

i. Display the results on a line graph. Use the axes below.

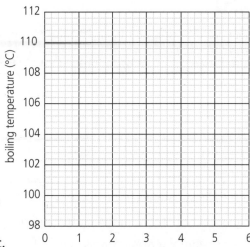

number of spoonfuls of salt

ii. On the graph, circle the anomalous result.

iii. Describe the pattern shown on the line graph.

....

....

iv. Suggest one improvement to the investigation.

....

1. Highlight the correct word or phrase in each **bold** pair in the paragraph below.

   When a substance melts, it changes state from **solid / liquid** to **solid / liquid**. During melting, the particles **move into/move out of** a regular pattern. The particles start to **vibrate on the spot / move around**. In both the solid and liquid state, the particles **are close to each other but do not touch / touch each other.** A substance has a high melting point if its particles hold together **weakly / strongly**.

TWS 2. The bar chart shows the melting point of six metals.

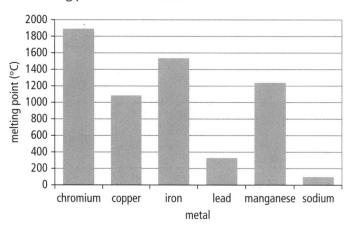

   a. Name the substance in the bar chart with the lowest melting point. ....

   b. List the substances in the bar chart in order of increasing melting point (lowest first).

   ....

   ....

TWS **c.** A scientist measures the melting point of an unknown metal as 1050 °C.
   Which metal on the bar chart is it most likely to be? ....

Extension

TWS The table gives melting points and boiling points of some substances.

Substance	Melting point (°C)	Boiling point (°C)
water	0	100
chlorine	−101	−34
bromine	−7.3	58
mercury	−39	357
ethanol	−114	78

   a. i. Name the substance in the table with the highest melting point. ....

   ii. Name the substance in the table with the highest boiling point. ....

   b. Draw a horizontal temperature scale for the temperatures in the table.
   Make sure the divisions on the scale are equal, and that the highest and lowest temperatures will fit.

   c. Mark the melting points and boiling points of the substances on your scale.

   d. i. Give the state of chlorine at 30 °C.

   ii. Give the state of ethanol at 20 °C.

TWS **iii.** Name the substance that is in the liquid state for the greatest temperature range.

Thinking and working scientifically

1. Circle the letter next to the *best* definition of a model in science.

   A. It is a smaller version of the real thing.

   B. It is an idea that explains observations.

   C. It is an idea that helps in making predictions.

   D. It is an idea that explains observations and helps in making predictions.

2. The particle model has strengths and limitations. For each statement, write a tick (✓) in the correct box in the table.

	This is a strength of the particle model	This is a limitation of the particle model	This can be a strength or a weakness
The particle model explains why some properties of a substance are different in the liquid and gas states.			
In the particle model, each particle is a sphere.			
The particle model cannot explain all properties.			
The particle model explains why different substances have different melting points.			
Some predictions made with the particle model are not correct.			
The particle model is simpler than reality.			

3. A teacher uses tomatoes to represent the particle model.

   Suggest how this model is better than, and worse than, representing the particle model in a drawing.

1. Write **T** next to the statements that are true. Write **F** next to the statements that are false. Then write corrected versions of the **three** false statements.

   a. Everything in the universe is made from the particles of one or more elements.

   b. An element is a substance that can be split up to make other substances.

   c. There are about 1000 elements.

   d. Each element has its own type of particle.

   e. In the periodic table, metals are on the right of the stepped line.

   Corrected versions of false statements:

   ....

   ....

   ....

2. The list below gives the names of some materials. Underline the names of the elements in the list. Use the periodic table on page 37 of the Student Book to help you.

wood	brass	bronze	glass	ruby	gold
copper	vanadium	iodine	oxygen	chlorine	salt

3. Write the names of the elements below in the correct column of the table.

lithium	manganese	nickel	oxygen	phosphorus	rhodium
sulfur	tungsten	vanadium	xenon	yttrium	zirconium

Metals	Non-metals

 4. Use information from pages 36–37 of the Student Book to give the names of:

   a. The two most common elements in the universe. ....

   b. The most common element in the atmosphere. ....

   c. An element that is in every living thing. ....

   d. An element that is used to make jewellery. ....

   e. An element that is used to make tools. ....

Extension

Use the Internet or a book to find out about two elements. For each element, explain how its properties make it suitable for its uses. If you are using the internet, search for *RSC periodic table* and then click on any of the elements shown.

2.2 Discovering the elements

Science in context

1. The table shows when some elements were discovered.

Time period	Some elements discovered in the time period
More than 3000 years ago	copper, silver, gold, iron, tin, lead, carbon, sulfur
1200–1699	zinc, platinum, arsenic, phosphorus
1700–1799	chromium, magnesium, nickel, hydrogen, nitrogen, oxygen, chlorine
1800–1899	potassium, sodium, calcium, aluminium, bromine, helium, iodine, silicon
1900–1999	rhenium, technetium

a. i. Name three elements that were discovered more than 3000 years ago.

....

ii. Explain why these elements were discovered so long ago.

....

....

b. i. Name four non-metal elements that were discovered in the 1700s.

....

ii. Suggest why these elements were not discovered earlier.

....

....

Extension

Read the information in the box.

The two discoveries of vanadium

In 1801, a professor in Mexico, Andrés Manuel del Río, investigated a local mineral. He thought there was a new element in the mineral. He experimented with the element. It joined with other elements to make substances of many colours. No other element had the same properties as the new element, but in some ways, it was like chromium. The professor called the new element *panchromium*.

The Mexican professor sent his mineral to France. A French scientist investigated it. He concluded that it contained the element chromium, and was not a new element.

In 1831, a Swedish professor, Nils Gabriel Sefström, investigated local samples of cast iron. Some broke easily. Others did not. The professor wondered why. He separated a new element from the stronger cast iron. He gave it a name – vanadium.

Later, a German scientist showed that *panchromium* and vanadium were the same. The professor in Mexico had discovered vanadium first, after all.

a. Explain why the Mexican professor thought he had discovered a new element.

....

b. Suggest why the Swedish professor did not know about the Mexican professor's discovery.

....

c. Identify one observation that led to the Swedish professor finding vanadium in some cast iron samples.

....

Thinking and working scientifically

1. In each list below, highlight the **one** chemical symbol that is written correctly.

   a. MG   mg   mG   Mg

   b. Be   BE   bE   be

   c. fE   FE   Fe   fe

2. Write the chemical symbol for each element in the table.

Name of element	chemical symbol
hydrogen	
helium	
lithium	
beryllium	
boron	
carbon	
nitrogen	
oxygen	
fluorine	
neon	

3. Write the names of the elements represented by the chemical symbols in the table.

Chemical symbol	Name of element
Na	
Mg	
Al	
Si	
P	
S	
Cl	
Ar	
K	
Ca	

4. Write the chemical symbols of each of the elements below. Then read the sentence.

   rhenium, vanadium, iodine, silicon, oxygen, nitrogen, iodine, sulfur, neon, cerium, sulfur, sulfur, argon, yttrium

Extension

Write down:

   a. The Japanese chemical symbol for phosphorus.

   b. The chemical symbol used by Chinese scientists for chlorine.

   c. The chemical symbol used by Latvian scientists for beryllium.

1. Write **T** next to the statements that are true. Write **F** next to the statements that are false.

   Then write corrected versions of the **three** false statements.

   a. An atom is the smallest part of an element that can exist.

   b. In science, a model is an idea that explains observations only.

   c. An element is a substance that is made from one type of atom.

   d. A single copper atom has the same properties as a block of copper.

   e. Every element has its own type of atom.

   f. Oxygen atoms are different from the atoms of every other element.

   g. The atoms of platinum and silver are identical.

   Corrected versions of false statements:

   ....

   ....

   ....

TWS 2. We can imagine atoms as spheres. In the diagrams, each circle represents one atom. Atoms of different elements have different shading.

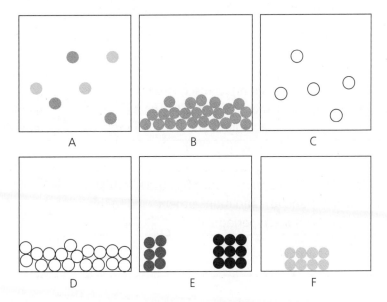

   a. Give the letters of **four** boxes that shows atoms of one element only. ....

   b. Give the letters of **two** boxes that each show atoms of two elements. ....

   c. Give the letters of **two** boxes that show atoms of the same element. ....

   d. Give the letters of **two** boxes that each show atoms of one of the elements in box A.

   ....

   e. Give the letters of **two** boxes that show atoms of the same element in different states.

   ....

Extension

If you could place one hundred million atoms side by side, they would stretch 1 cm. Calculate the number of atoms that would stretch 1 km.

Hint: There are 100 cm in 1 m, and 1000 m in 1 km.

Science in context

1. Scientific knowledge and understanding develops over time, as different scientists ask questions, and collect and consider their own and others' evidence.

   The flow diagram shows some of the steps in the development of the modern periodic table. Write the names or nationalities of one or two scientists in each box. Choose from the list below.

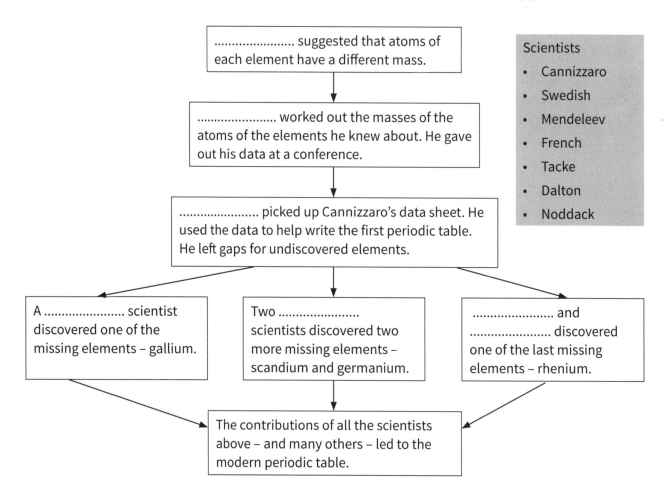

.... suggested that atoms of each element have a different mass.

.... worked out the masses of the atoms of the elements he knew about. He gave out his data at a conference.

.... picked up Cannizzaro's data sheet. He used the data to help write the first periodic table. He left gaps for undiscovered elements.

A .... scientist discovered one of the missing elements – gallium.

Two .... scientists discovered two more missing elements – scandium and germanium.

.... and .... discovered one of the last missing elements – rhenium.

The contributions of all the scientists above – and many others – led to the modern periodic table.

Scientists

- Cannizzaro
- Swedish
- Mendeleev
- French
- Tacke
- Dalton
- Noddack

Extension

Read the information in the box.

In 1875, a scientist called Boisbaudran discovered a new element. He called the element gallium. He measured its properties. Its density, he said, was 4.7 g/cm^3.

Boisbaudran realised that gallium was one of Mendeleev's 'missing elements'. Mendeleev had left a gap for it in his periodic table, and had predicted its properties. But there was a problem. Mendeleev had predicted that its density would be 5.9 g/cm^3. This didn't agree with Boisbaudran's value. So Boisbaudran checked his measurements and calculations. He had made a mistake. His corrected value was 5.96 g/cm^3.

a. Why did Boisbaudran check the density of his new element?

b. Boisbaudran's work showed that one of Mendeleev's predictions was correct. What effect might this have had on other scientists' opinions of the periodic table?

1. Highlight the correct **bold** words in the sentences below.

   A compound is a substance made up of atoms of **one / two / three** or more elements. The atoms are **strongly / weakly** joined together. The properties of a compound are **similar / different** to the properties of the elements whose atoms are in it. Some elements and compounds exist as molecules. A molecule is a particle made up of **one / two** or more atoms joined together **strongly / weakly.**

TWS 2. Water is a compound. It is made up of atoms of two elements, hydrogen and oxygen.

   Complete the table below.

Substance	Element or compound?	State at 20 °C	One property or use of the substance
hydrogen	element		
oxygen		gas	helps other substances to burn
water			

TWS

3. A student uses grapes and tomatoes to model molecules.

hydrogen molecule

water molecule

oxygen molecule

   a. Write the definition of a model in science.

   ....

   b. List some strengths and limitations of the model.

   Strengths:

   ....

   ....

   Weaknesses:

   ....

   ....

Extension

TWS The diagrams represent elements and compounds. Each circle represents one atom.

A   B   C   D

   a. Give the letters of the **two** diagrams that show compounds.

   b. Give the letters of the **two** diagrams that show molecules.

   c. Give the letter of **one** diagram that shows a compound in the solid state.

TWS **d.** Give the letter of **one** diagram that shows an element that exists as molecules.

2.7 What's in a name?

1. Give the names of the compounds made up of atoms of the elements below.

   a. magnesium and oxygen ....

   b. iron and sulfur ....

   c. aluminium and chlorine ....

   d. iron and bromine ....

   e. potassium and iodine ....

   f. sodium and nitrogen ....

2. The compounds below are each made up of atoms of three elements. For each compound, write the names of the three elements.

   a. calcium carbonate ....

   b. iron sulfate ....

   c. sodium nitrate ....

   d. potassium phosphate ....

3. Give the names of the compounds made up of atoms of the elements below.

   a. sodium, carbon, and oxygen ....

   b. magnesium, nitrogen, and oxygen ....

   c. copper, sulfur, and oxygen ....

4. Complete the table.

Molecule of compound made up of...	Name of compound
1 atom of carbon and 2 atoms of oxygen	
	carbon monoxide
1 atom of nitrogen and 2 atoms of oxygen	
	sulfur trioxide
1 atom of sulfur and 2 atoms of oxygen	

Extension

TWS Write the names of the compounds shown in the molecule diagrams below.

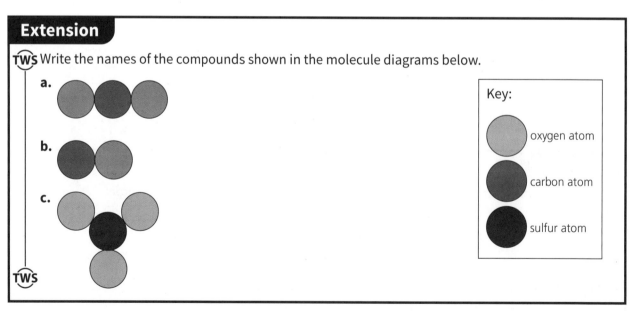

a.

b.

c.

Key:

oxygen atom

carbon atom

sulfur atom

TWS

Thinking and working scientifically

1. Write one number in each gap to complete the sentences below.

    a. The formula of sulfur dioxide is SO_2. This shows that there are .... oxygen atoms to every .... sulfur atom.

    b. The formula of nitrogen is N_2. This shows that a nitrogen molecule is made up of .... nitrogen atoms.

    c. The formula of water is H_2O. This shows that a water molecule is made up of .... hydrogen atoms joined to .... oxygen atom.

2. Draw lines to match each name to its formula.

Name
iodine
dinitrogen tetroxide
carbon monoxide
carbon dioxide
sulfur trioxide

Formula
CO
SO_3
I_2
N_2O_4
CO_2

3. Each formula below has one mistake. Write the formulae correctly.

    a. H2O   ....

    b. CO^2 ....

    c. $_2O$ ....

4. Complete the table below.

Name of compound	Relative number of atoms of each element	Formula
potassium iodide	1 potassium (K) to 1 iodine (I)	
lithium oxide	2 lithium (Li) to 1 oxygen (O)	
sodium nitrate	1 sodium (Na) to 1 nitrogen (N) to 3 oxygen (O)	
calcium sulfate	1 calcium (Ca) to 1 sulfur (S) to 4 oxygen (O)	
magnesium carbonate	1 magnesium (Mg) to 1 carbon (C) to 3 oxygen (O)	

Extension

Salbutamol is a compound. It is used to treat asthma. Its formula is $C_{13}H_{21}NO_3$.

a. Write the number of atoms of each element in one molecule of salbutamol.

b. Calculate the number of atoms of each element in five molecules of salbutamol.

1. Write **T** next to the statements that are true. Write **F** next to the statements that are false.

   Then write corrected versions of the **three** false statements.

   a. The different substances in a mixture are joined together.

   b. You cannot change the amounts of substances in a mixture.

   c. It is often easy to separate the substances in a mixture.

   d. In a mixture, the substances do not keep their own properties.

   e. Mixtures can contain elements only, or compounds only, or both.

   Corrected versions of false statements:

   ....

   ....

   ....

2. For each mixture, write a tick ✓ in the correct box in the table.

   Write **one** tick in each row.

Mixture	Mixture of elements only	Mixture of compounds only	Mixture of element(s) and compound
nitrogen and oxygen			
sodium chloride (salt) dissolved in water			
chlorine dissolved in water			
nitrogen, oxygen, and carbon dioxide			

TWS 3. In the diagrams below, each circle represents one atom. Circles with the same shading are atoms of the same element. Circles with different shading are atoms of different elements.

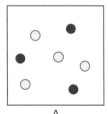 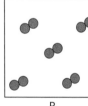 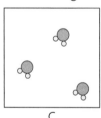 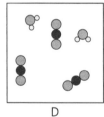 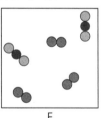

A   B   C   D   E

Give the letter of:

a. An element   ....

b. A compound   ....

c. A mixture of elements   ....

d. A mixture of compounds   ....

TWS

e. A mixture of an element and a compound   ....

Extension

A mixture includes substances with these formulae:

NaCl H_2O O_2 CO_2 KI   Mg

Is the mixture a mixture of elements, a mixture of compounds, or a mixture of elements and compounds?

1. Draw lines to match each word with its meaning.

Word	Meaning
solute	The process of adding a solid to a liquid so that you can no longer see separate pieces of solid.
solvent	A substance that dissolves in a liquid to make a solution.
solution	Able to dissolve.
dissolving	A mixture made when a substance dissolves in a liquid.
soluble	The liquid that a substance dissolves in.
insoluble	When a substance cannot mix with a liquid to make a solution.

2. Give the letter of the diagram below that best represents sugar dissolved in water.

Give a reason for your choice.

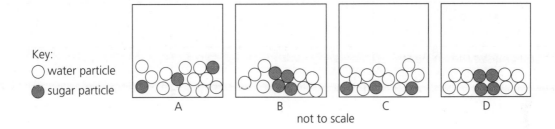

Key:
○ water particle
● sugar particle

A   B   C   D

not to scale

Reason: ....

3. James has 250 g of water. He adds 10 g of salt and stirs until it dissolves.

Calculate the mass of solution he makes.

....

Extension

A group of students adds 1 spatula measure of solid copper sulfate to water. They stir until the copper sulfate dissolves.

The students talk about their ideas.

Kamol: The solution is a mixture.

Lawan: The solution is a mixture of an element and a compound.

Mongkut: The mass of the solution is the mass of copper sulfate plus the mass of water.

Niran: Copper sulfate is insoluble in water.

Pakpao: Copper sulfate is the solvent.

Ratana: We could add another spatula measure of solid copper sulfate to the water and stir. If the solid disappears it has dissolved.

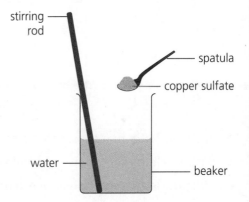

stirring rod
spatula
copper sulfate
water
beaker

a. Draw a table with two columns. Make the right column wider than the left column.

b. Write the names of the students in the left column.

c. In the right column, write whether each student's idea is correct or incorrect.

Write corrected versions of the incorrect statements.

2.11 Comparing elements, mixtures, and compounds

1. Highlight the correct **bold** words.

   Sodium has one type of atom, so it is **an element / a compound**. Sodium **can / cannot** be split into other substances. Chlorine is shown in the periodic table. It is **an element / a compound**. A teacher heats sodium in a Bunsen flame. He places the burning sodium in chlorine gas. This makes sodium chloride, which is **a compound / a mixture.** Sodium chloride has **similar / different** properties to the elements whose atoms are in it.

2. Complete the table to show some differences between compounds and mixtures.

	Mixtures of elements	Compounds
Can it easily be separated into its elements?		
How do its properties compare to those of its elements?		
Are its elements joined together?		
Can you change the amounts of each element in 100 g of the mixture or compound?		

TWS 3. The diagrams show particles in elements, mixtures, and compounds.

All the atoms of the same colour are atoms of the same element.

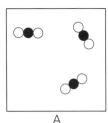
A

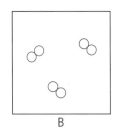
B

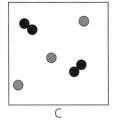
C

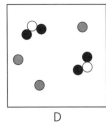
D

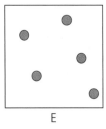
E

   a. Write the letter that shows atoms of one element. ....

   b. Write the letter that shows molecules of one element. ....

   c. Write the letter that shows molecules of one compound. ....

   d. Write the letter that shows a mixture of two elements. ....

   TWS e. Write the letter that shows a mixture of an element and a compound. ....

Extension

Write a paragraph to compare mixtures of elements and compounds. In the paragraph, describe how mixtures of elements and compounds are similar, and how they are different.

2.12 What are you made of?

1. Name the four elements that are present in the greatest amounts in your body.

   ....

2. Water is the compound that is present in the greatest amount in blood.
   Name the **two** elements that make up this compound.

   ....

3.

   a. Name the main compound in fingernails.

   ....

   b. Name the five elements that make up this compound.

   ....

SIG 4. Read the information in the box.

   > Iron is vital to humans. It is part of the compound haemoglobin in blood. Haemoglobin carries oxygen all over the body. The average amount of iron in the body is 3.8 g for men and 2.3 g for women.
   >
   > Many foods contain iron, including meat, beans, lentils, and dark green vegetables. If you do not have enough iron in your body, you may get anaemia. The symptoms of anaemia include tiredness, dizziness, and weakness. People with anaemia need to eat as much iron-rich food as possible. Doctors may suggest that a person with anaemia takes iron tablets.

   a. Give the average mass of iron in a woman.

   ....

   b. Name three foods that are rich in iron.

   ....

   c. Describe how iron is used in the body.

   ....

   d. List some symptoms of anaemia.

SIG

   ....

Extension

SIG Write a paragraph about mineral deficiency. Mention at least four minerals that you need. Describe the symptoms that you may have if you do not have enough of these minerals.

1. Circle the properties in the table below that are typical of metals in the solid state.

sonorous	shiny when freshly cut	brittle
high melting point	good conductor of thermal energy	strong
poor conductor of thermal energy	ductile	poor conductor of electricity
low melting point	good conductor of electricity	hard
dull	malleable	soft

SIC 2. Write down the property or properties that explain why metals are suitable for each use in the table.

Use	Properties that make metals suitable for this use
computer heat sinks	
bells	
bicycle frames	
electric cables	
cooking pans	
coins	
printed circuit boards	

SIC

Extension

TWS Read the information in the box, and study the bar chart.

Lithium, sodium, and potassium are metals. They are soft, like butter – you can easily cut them with a knife. They are shiny and silver-coloured when you first cut them, but they quickly get a white coating. Lithium, sodium, and potassium are good conductors of electricity.

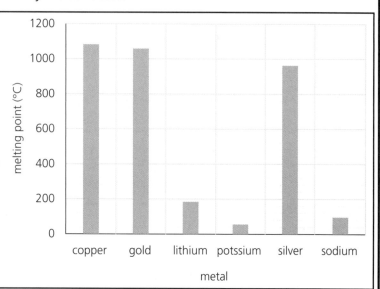

a. Write a sentence to describe what the data on the bar chart show.

b. Use the information in the box, the data on the bar chart, and your own knowledge, to list the ways that lithium, sodium, and potassium are typical metals, and the ways that they are not
TWS typical metals.

Thinking and working scientifically

1. Hassan has three spoons. Each is made of a different material. He asks a scientific question:

Which material conducts thermal energy best?

He sets up this apparatus.

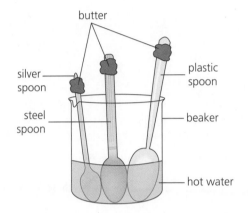

a. Hassan lists the variables in the investigation.

> Material the spoon is made of
> Size of spoon
> Time for butter to melt
> Amount of butter
> Temperature of water
> Distance from water to butter

Write each variable in the correct column of the table.

Type of variable	Variable in this investigation
independent	
dependent	
control	

b. Explain why Hassan cannot do a fair investigation with the apparatus shown.

....

c. Hassan adjusts his apparatus and carries out a fair test. He collects the data shown in the table.

Use the data to write a conclusion.

....

....

Material the spoon is made of	Time for butter to melt (seconds)
plastic	322
silver	30
steel	54

Extension

The table gives some data about five elements. All are in the solid state at 20 °C. Thermal conductivity is a measure of how well a substance conducts thermal energy. The higher the thermal conductivity, the better the substance conducts.

Name of element	Is the element a metal?	Thermal conductivity (W/m/K)
iodine	no	0.449
molybdenum	yes	138
niobium	yes	53.7
sulfur	no	0.205
technetium	yes	50.6

a. What conclusion can you make from the data in the table?

b. Carbon is a non-metal. One type of carbon has a thermal conductivity between 119 and 165 W/m/K. Does this data make you want to change your conclusion? If so, how? Give a reason for your decision.

1. Write **T** next to the statements that are true. Write **F** next to the statements that are false. Then write corrected versions of the **three** false statements.

   a. An alloy is a mixture of a metal with large amounts of other elements.

   b. An alloy has different properties to the elements in it.

   c. The alloy steel is mainly iron.

   d. Most alloys are less strong than the elements that are in them.

   e. Most alloys are softer than the elements that are in them.

   f. Stainless steel has different chemical properties to the elements that are in it.

   Corrected versions of false statements:

   ....

   ....

   ....

2. The diagrams show some atoms in pure iron and in steel. In the diagrams, the grey circles are iron atoms. The black circles are carbon atoms.

   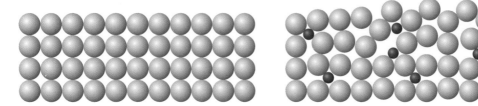

   a. Describe how the arrangements of iron atoms are different in pure iron and in steel.

   ....

   ....

   b. Explain how the difference in arrangement makes steel harder and stronger than pure iron.

   ....

   ....

Extension

TWS The table gives some data about pure titanium and a titanium alloy.

   a. Write a paragraph to compare the properties of the two materials.

   b. Explain the difference in strength of the two materials.

Property	Pure titanium	Alloy of: 90% titanium 6% aluminium 4% vanadium
Relative hardness (how easily the material scratches)	70	334
Strength, in MN/m² (the pulling force that breaks 1 m² of the material)	220	950
Appearance	shiny	shiny
TWS Is the material damaged when exposed to air and water?	no	no

1. The list below gives some properties. Highlight the properties that are typical of non-metals in the solid state.

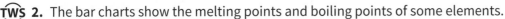

high melting point	brittle	poor conductor of thermal energy
strong	low melting point	shiny
poor conductor of electricity	dull	good conductor of electricity

TWS **2.** The bar charts show the melting points and boiling points of some elements.

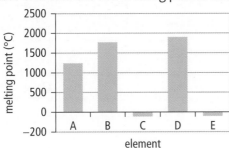 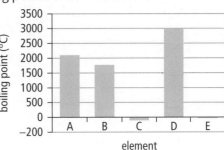

Each element is represented by a letter. The letters are not chemical symbols.

Use the bar charts to decide which elements are non-metals. Write their letters ....

3. The table gives some data about six elements. Each element is represented by a letter.

The letters are not chemical symbols.

Element	Melting point (°C)	Does the element conduct electricity?	Appearance of element in the solid state
G	2440	yes	shiny, silver coloured
H	3000	yes	shiny grey
I	44	no	white, not shiny
J	1769	yes	shiny, silver coloured
K	217	no	shiny, silver coloured
L	113	no	yellow, not shiny

a. Write the letters of the elements in order of increasing melting point.

Start with the lowest melting point...

TWS **b.** Give the letters of the three elements that are most likely to be metals.................................

Extension

TWS Read the information in the box, and study the data in the table.

> Germanium is an element. It is shiny and silvery-white. It is brittle.

Element	Metal or non-metal?	Electivity conductivity (Ω^{-1} m^{-1})
copper	metal	59 600 000
germanium	-	217
sulfur	non-metal	almost zero

a. Identify the properties of germanium that are similar to those of typical metals.

b. Identify one property of germanium that is similar to the properties of typical non-metals.

c. Germanium is classified as a *metalloid*. A metalloid is an element that has properties between those of
TWS metals and non-metals. Do you think this classification is appropriate? Give reasons for your decision.

1. Shade in the non-metals on the periodic table below.

							H hydrogen										He helium
Li lithium	Be beryllium											B boron	C carbon	N nitrogen	O oxygen	F fluorine	Ne neon
Na sodium	Mg magnesium											Al aluminium	Si silicon	P phosphorus	S sulfur	Cl chlorine	Ar argon
K potassium	Ca calcium	Sc scandium	Ti titanium	V vanadium	Cr chromium	Mn manganese	Fe iron	Co cobalt	Ni nickel	Cu copper	Zn zinc	Ga gallium	Ge germanium	As arsenic	Se selenium	Br bromine	Kr krypton
Rb rubidium	Sr strontium	Y yttrium	Zr zirconium	Nb niobium	Mo molybdenum	Tc technetium	Ru ruthenium	Rh rhodium	Pd palladium	Ag silver	Cd cadmium	In indium	Sn tin	Sb antimony	Te tellurium	I iodine	Xe xenon
Cs caesium	Ba barium	La lanthanum	Hf hafnium	Ta tantalum	W tungsten	Re rhenium	Os osmium	Ir iridium	Pt platinum	Au gold	Hg mercury	Tl thallium	Pb lead	Bi bismuth	Po polonium	At astatine	Rn radon
Fr francium	Ra radium																

Note: This periodic table does not include all the elements.

2. The diagram shows the atom arrangement in a metal element.

   a. Explain why most metals have high melting points.

   ....

   b. Explain why most metals are strong, particularly when mixed with other elements in alloys.

   ....

   ....

3. Iodine is made up of molecules, each with two iodine atoms.

   At 20 °C iodine is in the solid state, but its melting point is low.

   a. Explain why iodine has a low melting point.

   ....

   b. Explain why iodine is brittle.

   ....

Extension

TWS The table shows the thermal conductivity of six elements. The higher the thermal conductivity, the better an element conducts thermal energy. Each element is represented by a letter. The letters are not chemical symbols.

Element	Thermal conductivity (W/m/K
J	116
K	0.449
L	401
M	318
N	0.205
O	12.1

TWS Use the data to predict which of the six elements are metals. Explain your decisions.

Science in context

1. A company is choosing a new material for bicycle frames.
   Circle one property from each pair below that the material should have.

high density / low density	stiff / not stiff
hard / soft	shiny / dull
strong / weak	is not damaged by air and water / is damaged by air and water

2. Study the properties of materials **A**, **B**, and **C** in the table.

Property	Material A Alloy of: 95% titanium 3% aluminium 2% vanadium	Material B Alloy of: 90% titanium 6% aluminium 4% vanadium	Material C Pure titanium	Material D Alloy of: 98% aluminium 1.2% silicon 0.8% magnesium
Density, in g/cm³ (the higher the density, the heavier the bike for its size)	4.5	4.4	4.5	2.7
Relative hardness (how easily the material scratches)	256	334	70	30
Stiffness (GN/m²) (the greater the stiffness, the less bendy the material)	100	114	116	69
Fatigue strength (the smallest force that can damage the material) (MPa)	170	240	250	62
Appearance	shiny	shiny	shiny	shiny
Is the material damaged when exposed to air and water?	no	no	no	no

   a. Choose the best material to make bicycle frames, out of materials **A**, **B**, or **C** only. ....

   b. Explain your choice.

   ....

   ....

   c. Suggest one advantage of bamboo bicycle frames. ....

Extension

Imagine you work for a bicycle company. In the past, your company made bicycle frames from material **D** in the table above. Now it makes bicycles from a new material – your choice of **A**, **B**, or **C**. Make an advertisement to persuade people to buy bicycles made from the new material. You should:

- Explain the benefits of the new material, and why it is better than material **D**.
- Mention one disadvantage of the new material compared to material **D**.
- Tell people why you think the advantages of the new material outweigh this one disadvantage.

1. Use words and phrases from the box to complete the sentences below.

   Use each word once, more than once, or not at all.

substances	differently	similarly	rearrange	reverse
products	energy	reactants		

   A chemical reaction is a change that makes new .... In a chemical reaction, the

   atoms .... and join together .... Most chemical reaction are not easy

   to .... All chemical reactions transfer .... to or from the surroundings.

   The starting substances in a chemical reaction are .... The substances that are made

   are ....

2. Name the reactants and products in the chemical reactions.

Description of reaction	Reactant name(s)	Product name(s)
Magnesium reacts with oxygen to make magnesium oxide.		
Iron reacts with sulfur to make iron sulfide.		
Magnesium reacts with hydrochloric acid to make magnesium chloride and hydrogen.		
Sodium hydroxide reacts with copper sulfate to make copper hydroxide and sodium sulfate.		
On heating, copper carbonate makes copper oxide and carbon dioxide.		

TWS 3. A substance has this hazard symbol.

   a. Give the meaning of the hazard symbol. ....

   b. Suggest one safety precaution to take when working with the substance.

TWS

   ....

   ## Extension

   Zamira weighs a piece of magnesium. She burns the magnesium in oxygen.
   The reaction makes solid magnesium oxide. She weighs the magnesium oxide.

   The mass of magnesium oxide made is greater than the mass of magnesium at the start.
   Suggest why.

1. Write **T** next to the statements that are true. Write **F** next to the statements that are false.

   Then write corrected versions of the **two** false statements.

   Questions **c**, **d**, and **e** are about the reaction of hydrogen and oxygen, shown below:

   Two hydrogen ...react with... ...one oxygen ...to make... ...two water
   molecules...   molecule...   molecules.

   a. In a chemical reaction, the number of atoms of each element does not change.

   b. In a chemical reaction, the total mass of products may be greater than the total mass of reactants.

   c. When hydrogen reacts with oxygen, oxygen molecules split up.

   d. When hydrogen reacts with oxygen, hydrogen and oxygen atoms join together.

   e. A water molecule (H_2O) has one hydrogen atom joined to two oxygen atoms.

   Corrected versions of false statements:

   ....

   ....

2. The diagram shows how the atoms are rearranged and join together differently when nitrogen reacts with oxygen.

   Nitrogen...   ...reacts with...   ...oxygen ...   ...to make...   ...nitrogen monoxide.

   a. Give the number of nitrogen atoms shown in the reactants.   ....

   b. Give the number of nitrogen atoms shown in the products.   ....

   c. Give the number of oxygen atoms shown in the reactants.   ....

   d. Give the number of oxygen atoms shown in the products.   ....

   e. Write a conclusion based on your answers above. ....

   ....

Extension

Methane is a fuel. The diagram shows the reaction of methane and oxygen.

Describe how the atoms are rearranged and join together differently in the reaction.

Methane...   ...reacts   ...oxygen ...   ...to   ...carbon   ...and... ...water
with...   make...   dioxide...

Key:	⚪ Hydrogen atom	🔘 Oxygen atom	⚫ Carbon atom

Thinking and working scientifically

1. Read the definitions. Then write the correct words in the table.

   Choose from the words in the box.

prediction	hypothesis	conclusion

Definition	Word
A possible explanation that is based on evidence and that can be tested further.	
What you expect to happen in an investigation.	
A summary of what an investigation shows, with a scientific explanation.	

2. Farhad investigates copper carbonate. He makes some notes.

   - When you heat copper carbonate, it breaks down.
   - The products of the reaction are copper oxide and carbon dioxide.
   - Carbon dioxide leaves the test tube as it is made.
   - At room temperature:
     - copper carbonate is a green solid
     - copper oxide is a black solid
     - carbon dioxide is a colourless gas

   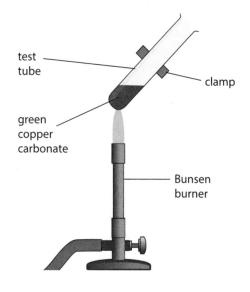

   Farhad sets up the apparatus opposite.

   a. Farhad weighs the test tube and its contents.
      mass of test tube = 25 g
      mass of test tube + copper carbonate = 27 g
      Calculate the mass of copper carbonate.

      ....

   b. Predict what Farhad will observe as he heats the copper carbonate.

      ....

   c. Farhad predicts that the mass of the test tube and contents will decrease. Suggest why.

      ....

   d. After heating, Farhad weighs the test tube and its contents.
      mass of test tube + product (copper oxide) after heating = 26 g
      Calculate the mass of copper oxide in the test tube.

      ....

   e. Calculate the mass of carbon dioxide gas made in the reaction.

      ....

   f. Write a conclusion for the experiment.

      ....

      ....

1. Draw lines to match each term to its definition.

Term	Definition
soluble substance	a substance that does not dissolve in a solvent
insoluble substance	a suspension of tiny solid particles in a liquid or solution
precipitate	a reaction in which two solutions react to make a precipitate
precipitation reaction	a reaction in which a substance reacts quickly with oxygen
combustion reaction	a substance that dissolves in a solvent

2. Name the precipitates that form when the pairs of solutions below react together.

   a. potassium iodide and lead nitrate ....

   b. copper chloride and sodium hydroxide ....

3. Ben has a compound. He does not know what it is.
   He dissolves the compound in water.
   He adds sodium hydroxide solution.
   A blue precipitate forms.
   Suggest the name of the metal in the compound.

   ....

 4. Give the meaning of each hazard symbol in the table.

Hazard symbol	Meaning

Extension

TWS For each hazard symbol in the table in question **4**, suggest one safety precaution you could take to reduce the risk of harm.

1. Highlight the correct **bold** word or phrase in each pair.

   Corrosion reactions happen **on the surface of / deep inside** a piece of metal. They gradually **damage / build up** the metal. Most corrosion reactions happen **slowly / quickly**.

   Iron corrodes when it reacts with **nitrogen / oxygen** from the air and water. The product of the corrosion reaction is **iron corrodite / rust**. This flakes off the surface of the iron and **exposes / hides** the iron atoms below so that they **can / cannot** react with more water and oxygen.

2. Draw lines from each type of property to statements that are true for that type of property.

Type of property	Statement
physical properties	how the substance takes part in chemical reactions
	for example, melting point
	properties you can observe or measure without changing a substance
chemical properties	for example, how quickly a substance corrodes or if it burns
	you can only find out about these by doing chemical reactions

SIC 3. The table lists some methods of preventing rusting.

   Draw a tick (✓) in one box next to each method to show how it works.

Method of preventing corrosion	Stops air and water touching the surface	Does not react with oxygen and water at all
covering with oil or grease		
making an alloy, such as stainless steel		
painting		
covering with a thin layer of zinc		

Extension

SIC The picture shows an iron ship that was made in the 1840s. It is now open for the public to visit. It is kept in a dry dock, so that people can walk underneath it.

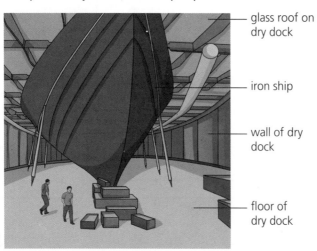

— glass roof on dry dock

— iron ship

— wall of dry dock

— floor of dry dock

a. The ship was abandoned under the sea in 1937. It was left there until about 1970. Explain why the ship went rusty.

b. Now, a machine dries the air in the dock. Suggest why.

1. In the table, write the names of three acidic substances and two alkaline substances.

Acidic substances	Alkaline substances

2. Some laboratory acids and alkalis are corrosive.

  a. Circle the hazard symbol below that means corrosive.

  b. List two things you can do to reduce risks from this hazard.

  ....

  ....

3. A student has some phenolphthalein indicator. She tests it in some solutions.

Her results are in the table.

Solution	Colour
hydrochloric acid	colourless
baking soda solution	pink
unknown solution	colourless

Is the unknown solution acidic or alkaline? ....

Give a reason for your decision.

....

Extension

A student collects petals from six different types of flower. Describe how they could find out which petals make good indicators. In your answer:

  • describe what they should do
  • explain how they would know which petals are suitable.

37

1. Write **T** next to the statements that are true. Write **F** next to the statements that are false.

    Then write corrected versions of the **three** statements that are false.

    a. A neutral solution has a pH of 7.0.

    b. An alkaline solution has a pH less than 7.0.

    c. The more acidic a solution, the higher its pH.

    d. If you dip red litmus paper into an alkaline solution, the paper becomes blue.

    e. You can use litmus paper to find out the pH of a solution.

    f. The higher the pH of a solution, the more alkaline it is.

    Corrected versions of false statements:

    ....

    ....

    ....

SIC 2. The pie chart shows the worldwide uses of sulfuric acid.

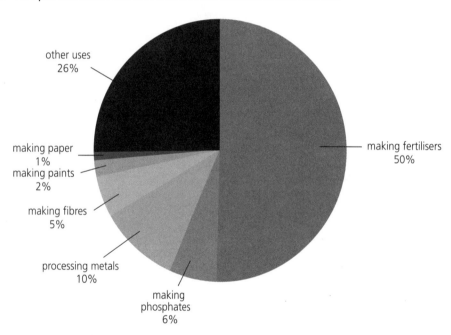

- Name the major use of sulfuric acid...

SIC • Give the percentage of sulfuric acid that is used to make paints..

Extension

A teacher dissolves 40 g of solid sodium hydroxide in water. She adds water to make 1000 cm³ of solution. This is solution A.

The teacher makes another solution by dissolving 20 g of sodium hydroxide in water. She adds water to make 1000 cm³ of solution. This is solution B.

Which is the more concentrated solution, A or B? Explain your decision.

1. Write **T** next to the statements that are true. Write **F** next to the statements that are false. Then write corrected versions of the **three** false statements.

   a. In a neutralisation reaction, an acid reacts with an alkali.

   b. If you add water to an acid, its concentration increases.

   c. Alex has an alkali of pH 12. He adds acid. The pH increases.

   d. If your soil is too acidic for a certain crop, add alkali to the soil to decrease its pH.

   e. Blessing has an acid of pH 2. She adds alkali. The pH increases.

   f. If your soil is too alkali for a certain crop, add acid to the soil to decrease its pH.

   Corrected versions of false statements:

   ....

   ....

   ....

2. Circle the correct **bold** words and numbers.

   Som has some sodium hydroxide solution. He adds universal indicator. The colour of the mixture is **green / purple / red**. This shows that sodium hydroxide solution is **acidic / alkaline / neutral**.

   Som adds a little hydrochloric acid to the sodium hydroxide solution. The pH **decreases / increases**. He adds more hydrochloric acid. Eventually the solution is neutral. Its pH is **1 / 7 /14**. The acid has **neutralised / oxidised** the sodium hydroxide solution.

   Som adds even more acid. The pH **decreases / increases**. The mixture is acidic. Its colour is **green / purple / red**.

Extension

TWS A student has the apparatus and solutions shown here. The two solutions have the same concentration. The student pours the sodium hydroxide into the acid. The indicator changes colour. Give the letter of the one correct results table.

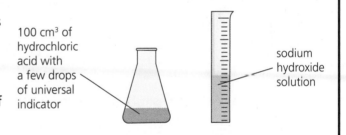

100 cm³ of hydrochloric acid with a few drops of universal indicator

sodium hydroxide solution

A.

volume of alkali (cm³)	indicator colour	pH
0	green	7
100	red	1

B.

volume of alkali (cm³)	indicator colour	pH
0	red	1
100	blue	14

C.

volume of alkali (cm³)	indicator colour	pH
0	red	1
TWS 100	green	7

Thinking and working scientifically

1. Read the information in the box, then answer the questions below.

> Mbuyu School has a pond. Its plants and animals are dying. Students test the water. The water is too acidic. The caretaker wants to neutralise the extra acid so that the pondwater pH is 7. He decides to add limestone powder to the pond. He needs to know how much to buy. He asks some students to investigate.

   a. The students think of questions to investigate. They have three ideas:

   A. What mass of limestone will increase the water pH to 7.0?

   B. What mass of limestone will keep the animals alive?

   C. What mass of limestone will cover the pond bed to a depth of 10 cm?

   The students decided to investigate question **A**. Explain why this question is most suitable.

   ....

   ....

   b. The students plan to add limestone to samples of pond water. They will stir the mixture and measure the new pH. The students list the variables in the investigation:

   - volume of water in sample
   - mass of limestone
   - pH after adding limestone
   - speed and time of stirring
   - pH before adding limestone

   i. Give the independent variable. ....

   ii. Give the dependent variable. ....

   iii. The students keep the other three variables constant. Explain why.

   ....

   c. The students do the investigation. They collect the evidence in the table below.

Mass of limestone (g)	pH after adding limestone
5	5.0
10	5.5
15	5.6
20	7.0
25	7.0
30	7.0

   i. Suggest the best mass of limestone to add to the pond, if the amount of water in the pond is the same as the amount of water in the sample. Explain your decision.

   ....

   ....

   ii. Identify one other piece of data the students need before telling the caretaker how much limestone to buy.

   ....

Science in context

1. The list shows some causes and effects of acid rain:
   - Write **C** next to the causes.
   - Write **E** next to the effects.
   a. Waste gases from some factories ....
   b. Damages some buildings ....
   c. Burning coal ....
   d. Makes lakes acidic ....
   e. Kills trees ....
   f. Chemical reactions in car engines ....
   g. Burning rubbish ....

2. Limestone rock is mainly calcium carbonate. Some acid rain contains nitric acid. When this acid rain falls on limestone, there is a chemical reaction:

nitric acid	...reacts with...	calcium carbonate	...to make...	calcium nitrate	...and...	water	and	carbon dioxide
(colourless solution in acid rain)		(solid limestone or marble)		(colourless solution)		(liquid)		(colourless gas)

   a. Give the names of the reactants in the chemical reaction.

   ....

   b. Give the names of the products in the chemical reaction.

   ....

Extension

Think about what you can do to reduce acid rain. Write down your ideas.

Then talk about your ideas with someone at home.

Changes I can make in my own life to make to make less acid rain.

Changes I can ask my family to make to make less acid rain.

Things I can do to influence my community to make less acid rain, or to reduce its effect.

Things I can ask the government to do to help people make less acid rain, or to reduce its effects.

1. This question is about gas tests.

   a. Colour each box about carbon dioxide **grey**.

   b. Colour each box about oxygen **red**.

   c. Leave each box about hydrogen **white**.

Gas	Chemical formula	Test	Expected observation
carbon dioxide	CO_2	lighted splint	flame goes out with a squeaky pop
hydrogen	O_2	limewater	goes milky
oxygen	H_2	glowing splint	splint relights

2. Look at the information about two chemical reactions.

   Then write the names of the reactants and products of each reaction in the table below.

Chemical reaction A

hydrochloric ...reacts calcium ...to calcium ...and... water ...and... carbon
acid with... carbonate make... chloride dioxide

Chemical reaction B

zinc ...reacts with... hydrochloric acid ...to make... zinc chloride ...and... hydrogen

Reaction	Names of reactants	Names of products
A		
B		

Extension

Choose one of these substances: carbon dioxide, hydrogen, and oxygen.

Use the Internet to find out about the properties and uses of the substance.

For hydrogen and oxygen, search for *RSC periodic table* and click on the symbols of the elements. For carbon dioxide, search for *properties and uses of carbon dioxide*.

Science in context

1. Label the diagram of the Earth by writing one or two words in each box.

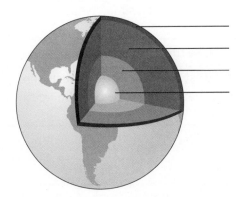

2. For sentences **a** to **g** below:

Write **C** next to the sentences that are true for the Earth's crust.

Write **M** next to the sentences that are true for the mantle.

Write **O** next to the sentences that are true for the outer core.

Write **I** next to the sentences that are true for the inner core.

You will need to write more than one letter next to some sentences.

a. This is at the centre of the Earth. ....

b. This part of the Earth is solid. ....

c. This part of the Earth is liquid. ....

d. This part of the Earth is made up mainly of iron and nickel. ....

e. This part of the Earth can flow. ....

f. This part of the Earth is made up of different types of rock. ....

g. This part of the Earth has the smallest thickness. ....

3. Write down three pieces of evidence that support the idea that the Earth is not flat, but that it is a sphere.

1. ....

2. ....

3. ....

Extension

A scientist named Inge Lehmann discovered the inner core in 1936.

Use the Internet to find out about the life and work of Inge Lehmann.

Make a poster or write about what you have found out. You could include information about:

- where she lived
- her school and universities
- how she found out about the inner core
- things that have been named after her
- how long she lived.

---

1. Draw lines to show whether each statement is:

   - *either* evidence for plate tectonics

   - *or* a reason that other scientists rejected the idea of plate tectonics at first.

	Scientists found fossils of the same animal in Africa and South America.
evidence for plate tectonics	Scientists did not know *how* the continents could move.
	Some scientists did not trust Wegener (the scientist who suggested the hypothesis) because he mainly studied the weather, not rocks.
reason that other scientists rejected the idea of plate tectonics at first	Scientists found fossils of the same plants in Africa and South America.
	The shapes of Africa and South America look as if they fit together.

SIC 2. Scientists build on each other's evidence and ideas. They share and discuss evidence and ideas in different ways.

In the list below, highlight ways that scientists communicate now that they could not have used 50 years ago.

   a. Face-to-face conversations

   b. Text message

   c. Email

   d. Giving talks at conferences

   e. Writing about their work for scientific journals

SIC f. Shared web pages

Extension

Use the Internet to find out about the life and work of Alfred Wegener.

Make a poster or write about what you have found out. You could include information about:

- the expeditions he went on

- his work on continental drift

- interesting things about his life.

1. The steps below describe how an earthquake may happen, and some of its impacts.

   Write the letters of the steps in a sensible order. The first one has been done for you.

   A. At some plate boundaries, the plates are sliding past each other.

   B. Suddenly, the two plates overcome the frictional forces.

   C. Collapsing buildings may kill people.

   D. The two plates slip suddenly. This is an earthquake.

   E. Sometimes the two plates get stuck.

   F. Shock waves make buildings collapse.

   G. Because of friction, the plates do not slide past each other smoothly.

   H. When the plates are stuck, big forces build up.

   I. Shock waves spread from where the plates slip.

   Correct order:

A								

2. The map shows the Andes mountains in South America. The arrows show the movement of two tectonic plates – the Nazca plate and the South American plate.

   Use the diagrams to suggest an explanation for how the Andes mountains formed.

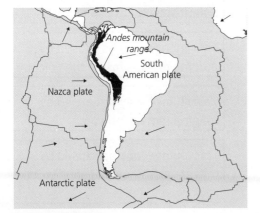

   ....

   ....

   ....

   ....

   ....

   ....

   ....

   ....

Extension

Read the information in the box.

> Earthquakes send out shock waves. There are two types of shock waves:
> - P-waves, which travel through solids and liquids
> - S-waves, which travel through solids but not through liquids.
>
> During earthquakes, scientists use seismometers to try to detect P-waves and S-waves in different places. This helps them to find out about the structure of the Earth.

The diagram shows the centre of an earthquake, and the beginnings of paths of some shock waves from the earthquake. Assume the waves travel in straight lines.

Write the letters of the places where you predict scientists would detect:

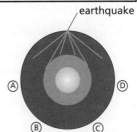

a. P-waves only

b. S-waves and P-waves.

1. Write **T** next to the statements that are true. Write **F** next to the statements that are false.

   Then write corrected versions of the **three** false statements.

   a. A volcano is an opening in the Earth's crust that liquid rock and other materials escape from.

   b. Most volcanoes are at plate boundaries.

   c. At plate boundaries, rock can get hot enough to melt.

   d. Lava is liquid rock that is under the ground.

   e. Magma is liquid rock that is above ground.

   f. Some volcanoes form at hot spots, where heat melts rock in the mantle.

   g. There are about 5 million active volcanoes in the world.

   Corrected versions of false statements:

   ....

   ....

   ....

2. Draw lines to match each prediction with a suitable scientific explanation.

   One of the explanations explains two predictions.

Prediction
When the steepness of a volcano slope changes, the volcano may erupt.
When there are more frequent earth movements near a volcano, the volcano may erupt.
Magma often contains dissolved sulfur dioxide. When extra sulfur dioxide gas comes out of a volcano, the volcano may erupt.
When the surface temperature of a volcano changes, the volcano may erupt.

Scientific explanation
This change may be caused by magma moving inside the volcano.
This change may be caused by magma moving upwards.
This change may be caused by magma pushing up against surface rock.

Extension

TWS Scientists studied data from 3200 volcanic eruptions between the years 1700 and 1999.

Some students read about their work and wrote down their ideas.

Kibibi: There were more violent volcanic eruptions between November and March than during the other months of the year.

Lisimba: I live near a volcano. I think its next eruption will be between November and March.

Muna: More snow and rain fall on the northern half of the Earth between November and March. This pushes down on the Earth's surface rock. I think that the extra force makes magma move in volcanoes.

a. Give the name of the person who is making a prediction. ....

b. Give the name of the person who is suggesting an explanation for the data. ....

TWS c. Give the name of the person who is describing a pattern in data. ....

1. Until the early 1900s, scientists modelled atoms as solid spheres. Draw one tick (✓) in each row of the table to show what the solid sphere model can, and cannot, explain.

Phenomenon	The solid sphere model of atoms *can* explain this.	The solid sphere model of atoms *cannot* explain this.
condensing		
chemical reactions		
melting		

2. Scientists now know that atoms are made up of sub-atomic particles.

   Use words from the box to label the diagram of the lithium atom below. A lithium atom has three protons.

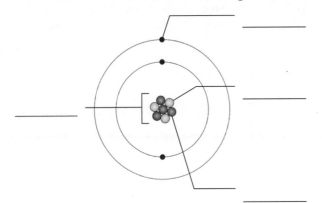

nucleus

electron

neutron

proton

3. **a.** A boron atom has 5 protons and 6 neutrons. Give its number of electrons. ....

   a. A potassium atom has 20 neutrons and 19 electrons. Give its number of protons. ....

   b. A nickel atom has 28 protons and 31 neutrons. Give its number of electrons. ....

   c. An arsenic atom has 33 electrons and 42 neutrons. Give its number of protons. ....

4. Draw diagrams of the nuclei of the atoms in the boxes below.

A carbon nucleus made up of 6 protons and 6 neutrons.	A beryllium nucleus made up of 4 protons and 5 neutrons.	A fluorine nucleus made up of 9 protons and 10 neutrons.

Extension

TWS The statement in the box below is an analogy.

> **An atom is like a tomato, with its pips (seeds) representing electrons.**

Evaluate this analogy. In your answer, describe how a tomato is like an atom, and how it is unlike TWS the 1932 model of an atom. Then make a judgement about the overall usefulness of the analogy.

Thinking and working scientifically

1. The scientist J. J. Thomson investigated cathode rays.

   Draw one line from each investigation part to the scientist's statement.

Part of investigation	Scientist's statement or question
scientific question	Cathode rays move towards a positive electrode, so they might have a negative electrical charge.
hypothesis	Cathode rays are charged. Their charge is negative.
prediction	What are cathode rays?
conclusion	If I pass cathode rays between electrically charged pieces of metal, the rays will change direction. The rays will bend towards the positively-charged metal.

2. J. J. Thomson and another scientist, Nagaoka, developed different models for the structure of an atom. The table gives some information about the two models.

Part of model	J. J. Thomson (plum pudding model)	Nagaoka
positive charge	Atoms are made up of a positively-charged sphere, which is the size of the whole atom.	Atoms have a positively charged centre, which is smaller than the atom. Most of the mass of the atom is in the nucleus.
negative charge	Electrons are placed throughout the sphere.	Electrons orbit outside the centre of the atom in rings, like the planet Saturn.

   a. Describe two ways in which the models are similar to each other.

   ....

   ....

   b. Describe one way in which the models are different to each other.

   ....

   ....

Extension

The statement in the box below is an analogy for Thomson's model of the atom.

> **An atom is like a watermelon, with its pips (seeds) representing electrons.**

Evaluate this analogy. In your answer, describe how a watermelon is like Thomson's model of an atom, and how it is unlike this model of an atom. Then make a judgement about the overall usefulness of the analogy.

Science in context

1. In 1909 Geiger and Marsden fired positively-charged particles at gold foil.
   The diagram shows some of their observations. Each arrow is the path of one particle.

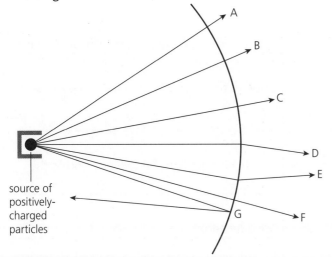

Write the letters of the lines in the correct boxes.

Lines that show...	Letters
...the paths of four particles that travel straight through the foil.	
...the paths of two particles that change direction a little.	
...the path of one particle that bounces backwards off the foil.	

2. For the experiment in question **1**, draw one line from each observation to the correct explanation.

Observation
Most particles travel straight through the foil.
A very few particles bounce backwards off the foil.
Some particles change direction a little as they travel through the foil.

Explanation
These particles hit a positively-charged nucleus.
These particles travel through the empty space between nuclei.
These particles travel close to a positively-charged nucleus.

Extension

Scientists built on each other's work to discover the structure of the atom.
Write the letter of one discovery next to each date on the timeline.

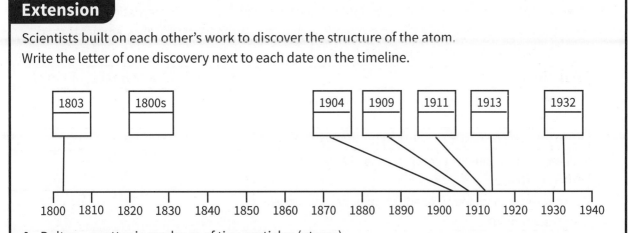

A. Dalton – matter is made up of tiny particles (atoms)

B. Geiger and Marsden – gold foil experiment

C. Rutherford – atoms have a nucleus and electrons orbit outside the nucleus

D. Curie and Rutherford – conference to discuss models for atoms

E. Several scientists – gas investigation

F. Thomson – plum pudding model

G. Chadwick – discovers neutrons

Science in context

1. The statements in the boxes on the left describe how scientists investigated what gives protons and neutrons their mass.

   a. Draw lines to match each statement to one stage of developing a scientific explanation.

What scientists did	Stage of developing a scientific explanation
Suggested that there is a particle (Higgs boson) that gives protons and neutrons their mass. Described properties of the Higgs boson.	**A** Use creative thought to make a hypothesis
Built the Large Hadron Collider and made protons collide in it. Observed the products of the collisions.	**B** Decide whether the evidence supports the hypothesis
Wondered what gives protons and neutrons their mass.	**C** Ask a question
Compared the products of the collisions with the predicted properties of the Higgs boson.	**D** Collect evidence

   b. Write the letters of the stages in a sensible order.

   ....

2. Today, many scientists work in international teams.

   a. Suggest why scientists are more likely to work in international teams in the 21st century than in the 19th century.

   ....

   b. The statements below are advantages and disadvantages of working in international teams. Write **A** next to the advantages and **D** next to the disadvantages. Write **B** next to any statements that could be both an advantage and a disadvantage.

Statement	Advantage, disadvantage, or both?
In an international team, scientists may speak different languages.	
In an international team, costs can be shared.	
Scientists from different countries may be experts in different things.	
In an international team, scientists may not meet their colleagues often.	

1. Draw lines to make three correct definitions.

Proton number is	the total number of protons and neutrons in an atom.
Mass number is	the number of protons in an atom.
Nucleon number is	

2. Use the periodic table on page 6 to help you answer this question.

   Write the chemical symbol of each element in the box below its proton number.

75	23	53	14	8	7	53	16	9	92	7
									U	

   Now crack the code. What does the sentence say?

   ....

3. Complete the table below.

Atom of the element...	Proton number	Number of neutrons	Nucleon number
hydrogen	1		1
	2	2	
	4		9
	7	7	
	11		23
	16	16	
titanium	22	26	

4. Write the missing number or name in each sentence below.

   a. The mass of a carbon atom is .... times the mass of a helium atom.

   b. The mass of a helium atom is .... times the mass of a hydrogen atom.

   c. The mass of a .... atom is twice the mass of a nitrogen atom.

   d. The mass of a .... atom is five times of the mass of a nitrogen atom.

   e. The mass of an oxygen atom is .... the mass of a sulfur atom.

   f. The mass of a calcium atom is twice the mass of a .... atom.

1. Circle the correct **bold** words and phrases in the sentences below.

   A pure substance has **one type** / **many types** of particle/s. The only pure substances are **elements / elements and compounds**. In science, a pure substance **has nothing mixed with it / is natural**. A substance has particles with the formula $C_8H_9NO_2$. It **is / is not** pure because it has atoms of more than one element.

TWS 2. Rajeev sets up this apparatus. Samples **A** and **B** are hot, and in the liquid state.

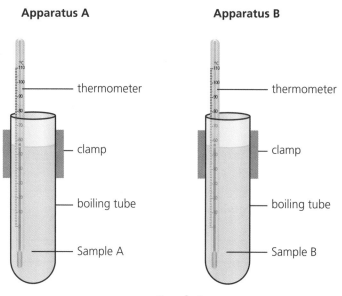

Rajeev allows the samples to cool. He measures their temperature every minute. He plots the graphs below.

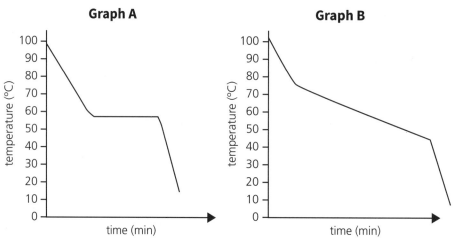

   a. Write a conclusion for the experiment to answer this scientific question:

      *Which sample, **A** or **B**, is a pure substance?*

      In your conclusion, give the answer to the question and the evidence for it.

      ....

      ....

   TWS **b.** Estimate the melting point of the pure substance. .... °C

   Extension

   Write a paragraph to compare pure and impure substances. Include:

   a. how pure and impure substances are similar

   b. how pure and impure substances are different.

Science in context

1. Draw lines to match each part of seawater to the scientific word that describes it.

Part of seawater
salt
seawater
water

Scientific word
solvent
solute
solution

2. Use words from the box to complete the sentences below. Use each word once, more than once, or not at all.

seawater	evaporates	pure	condenses	freezes

Desalination is used to obtain .... water from .... One method of desalination

is distillation. Distillation involves heating .... Pure water .... to make steam.

The steam travels through a condenser, where it cools and ....

3. The diagram shows laboratory distillation apparatus. Label the apparatus using the words and phrases in the box.

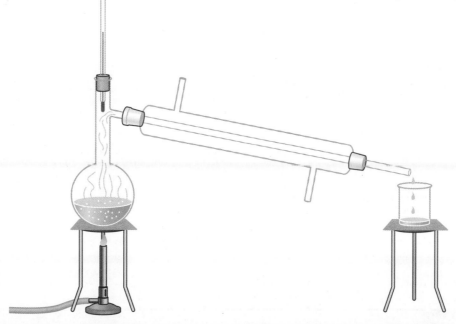

seawater	pure water	beaker	condenser
round-bottomed flask	tap water in	tap water out	

Extension

Suggest why tap water is not obtained by desalination in places where it rains a lot.

TWS 1. Sarah has a piece of an unknown leaf. She wants to know if the leaf is from a spinach plant or a cassava plant. She has this apparatus.

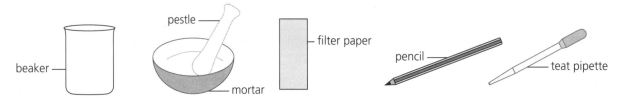

The stages below describe what to do. They are in the wrong order. Write the letters in a sensible order. The first one has been done for you.

A. Pour solvent into the bottom of the beaker. Stand the paper in the beaker.

B. Use a pestle and mortar to crush three leaves – the unknown leaf, a spinach leaf, and a cassava leaf.

C. Wait as the solvent moves up the paper.

D. Draw a pencil line on the chromatography paper.

E. Take out the paper. Compare the patterns.

F. Put one spot of liquid from each leaf on the pencil line.

B					

2. The chromatogram shows ink from three pens.

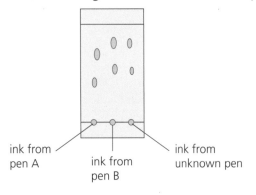

ink from pen A

ink from pen B

ink from unknown pen

a. Is the unknown pen the same as pen A or pen B?

....

Explain your choice.

....

....

TWS

3. Describe three uses of chromatography.

....

....

....

Extension

Use words from the box to complete the sentences below. Use each word once, more than once, or not at all.

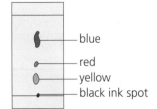

blue

red

yellow

black ink spot

blue	chromatography
yellow	red
most	least
chromatogram	three
four	two

This is a .... of black ink. It shows that the black ink is a mixture of .... coloured inks. The .... ink has moved furthest. This might be because this ink is .... soluble in water. Or it might be that this ink sticks .... strongly to the paper.

1. Write **T** next to the statements that are true. Write **F** next to the statements that are false. Then write corrected versions of the **three** false statements.

   a. Concentration is a measure of the number of solute particles in a volume of solution.

   b. A dilute solution has few solute particles in 100 cm³ of solution.

   c. A concentrated solution has many solute particles in 100 cm³ of a solution.

   d. To make a solution more concentrated, add more solvent.

   e. To make a solution more dilute, add more solute.

   f. The more solute particles in 100 cm³ of solution, the more dilute the solution.

   Corrected versions of false statements:

   ....

   ....

   ....

2. The diagrams show two solutions.

   Circle the more concentrated solution.

   Solution A   Solution B

   Key:
   ● Solute particle
   ○ Solvent particle

   Not to scale

3. In the beaker, draw the particles in a solution that is more concentrated than solution B in question **2**.

Extension

TWS You can use the formula below to calculate the concentration of a solution.

$$\text{concentration} = \frac{mass\ of\ solute}{volume\ of\ solution}$$

In each pair, highlight the more concentrated solution.

	Solution X	Solution Y
a.	100 g of salt in 100 cm³ of solution	200 g of salt in 100 cm³ of solution
b.	100 g of salt in 100 cm³ of solution	100 g of salt in 200 cm³ of solution
c.	100 g of salt in 100cm³ of solution	400 g of salt in 200 cm³ of solution
d.	100 g of salt in 100 cm³ of solution	100 g of salt in 50 cm³ of solution
TWS e.	100 g of salt in 100 cm³ of solution	100 g of salt in 500 cm³ of solution

Thinking and working scientifically

1. Moyo has a sample of rock salt. He wants to find the mass of salt in his sample.

   Rock salt is a mixture of salt (sodium chloride) and rock.

   a. First, Moyo finds the mass of his rock salt.

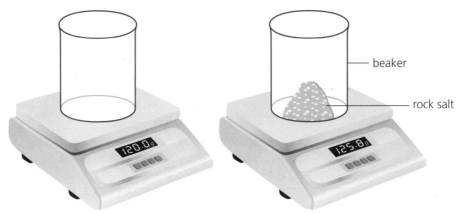

   Use the data in the drawings to complete the table.

	Mass (g)
mass of empty beaker	
mass of beaker + rock salt	
mass of rock salt	

   b. Moyo grinds the rock salt in a pestle and mortar.
   He adds water to dissolve the salt. The rock does not dissolve.
   He filters the mixture. He now has a solution of salt in water.

   The sentences below describe what Moyo does next. They are in the wrong order. Write the letters of the stages in a sensible order. The first one has been done for you.

   A. Find the mass of an evaporating basin.

   B. Leave the solution in a warm dry place.

   C. Use a Bunsen burner to heat the salt solution until half the water has evaporated.

   D. When all the water has evaporated, find the mass of the evaporating basin and its contents.

   E. Pour the solution into the evaporating basin.

   F. Calculate the mass of salt.

A					

   c. Complete the risk assessment for the experiment.

Hazard	Risk from hazard	Reduce chance of injury and damage by...
hot apparatus	burns to skin	
salt spitting from boiling salty water		

   d. Another student, Mapiro, has a sample of the same rock salt. Both students have the same mass of rock salt. Mapiro uses the same method as Moyo to separate salt from his sample. The mass of salt in Mapiro's sample is less. Suggest two reasons for this difference.

Science in context

As you know, adding chlorine to water helps to make it safe to drink. In some places, water companies also add fluorine compounds to water. The information in the box describes an investigation about adding a fluorine compound to water. Read the information, and then answer the questions below it.

Fluoridation of drinking water

In some places, water companies add fluorine compounds to water. The purpose of adding these compounds is to protect against tooth decay. A few years ago, two scientists asked a question. Did the fluoridation of water in New Zealand towns affect tooth decay in children?

The scientists collected evidence. In 2007 they examined the teeth of 540 5–6 year olds and 12–13 year olds from four towns. Two of the towns then started fluoridating their water. In 2009, the scientists examined the teeth of 514 children of the same ages in the same towns.

The table below summarises some of the evidence collected.

Town	Was the water fluoridated?	Change from 2007 to 2009 in number of 5–6 year olds with teeth missing because of decay	Change from 2007 to 2009 in number of 12–13 year olds with decayed, missing or filled teeth	Change in number of 12–13 year olds with surface tooth decay detected by x-rays
A	yes	decreased	decreased	decreased
B	no	increased	decreased	no change
C	yes	decreased	no change	decreased
D	no	decreased	no change	no change

---

1. The scientists collected evidence from more than 500 people in both 2007 and 2009. Suggest why they used a large number of people.

   ....

2. Suggest why the scientists collected evidence from two towns with fluoridated water and two towns without fluoridated water.

   ....

3. The scientists said that it would have been better to collect data from 2007 and 2012 (not from 2007 to 2009). Suggest how this might have improved the investigation.

   ....

4. Use the data in the table to write a conclusion for the investigation.

   ....

   ....

5. The scientist discovered that, for several months between 2007 and 2009, the water companies in towns A and C did not add enough fluoride to the water. Write a new conclusion for the investigation that takes account of this discovery.

   ....

   ....

1. You can obtain solubility data from secondary sources.

   Highlight the **three** secondary sources that are most likely to be trustworthy.

   A. university chemistry department web site

   B. a group chat

   C. chemistry data book

   D. report of a chemistry experiment written by a school student

   E. chemistry text book

 2. The table shows the solubility of some salts at 20 °C.
   Use the data to plot a bar chart.
   Use the axes below.

Salt	Solubility (g/100 g of water)
magnesium chloride	54
calcium chloride	75
strontium chloride	54
barium chloride	36

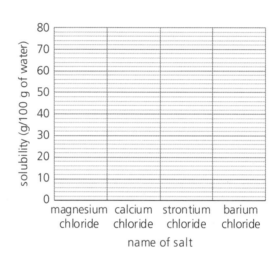

Extension

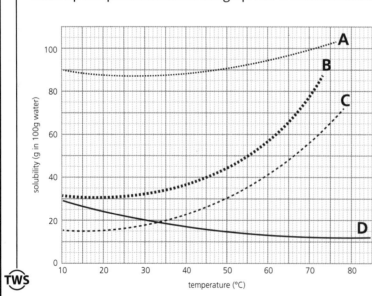 The graph shows how solubility changes with temperature for four salts – **A**, **B**, **C**, and **D**.
Make up six questions about the graph for a friend to answer.

Thinking and working scientifically

1. Vazir plans to investigate dissolving. He thinks of a question to answer:

How does water temperature affect the mass of salt that dissolves?

a. Draw lines to identify the variables in the investigation.

Type of variable
independent
dependent
control

Variable
volume of water
water temperature
mass of salt

b. From each pair below, circle the more suitable piece of apparatus.

i. To measure the volume of water.

ii. To measure the temperature of the water.

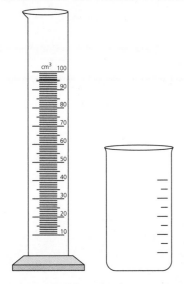

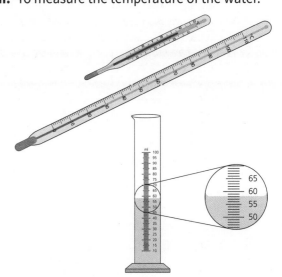

c. Give the volume of water in the measuring cylinder.

.... cm³

d. Before starting the investigation, Vazir writes down what he will do. He misses out some steps. Write the missing steps on the answer lines.

A. Measure out 100 cm³ of water and pour it into a beaker.

B. ....

C. Add salt, 1 g at a time, while stirring.

D. When no more will dissolve, write down the mass of salt added.

E. ....

F. Heat the water to 40 °C.

G. Add salt, 1 g at a time, while stirring.

H. ....

Thinking and working scientifically

1. Nadira investigates the time taken for sugar with different sized grains to dissolve in water. She writes her results in a table.

Size of grains	Time for 50 g of sugar to dissolve in 100 g of water (s)
small	18
medium	40
big	61

Plot her results on a bar chart.

2. Tahira uses a secondary source to find the solubility of a salt at different temperatures. She writes the data in a table.

Temperature (°C)	Mass of the salt that dissolves in 100 g of water (g)
10	8
20	12
30	16
40	20
60	39
80	60

a. Plot the data on a line graph.

b. Why should the results be plotted on a line graph, not a bar chart?

   Choose the best answer from the statements below.

   A. The independent variable is discrete but the dependent variable is continuous.

   B. The independent variable is continuous but the dependent variable is discrete.

   C. The independent and dependent variables are discrete.

   D. The independent and dependent variables are continuous.

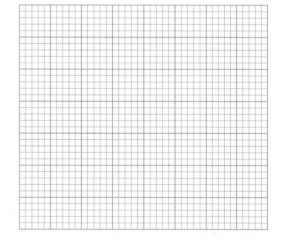

Extension

Khalid measures the solubility of three substances in water at six temperatures.
The substances are copper sulfate, sodium carbonate, and potassium chloride.
Draw one table in which he can write all his results.

1. Write four correct sentences about chemical reactions using the phrases in the table.

   Each sentence must include a phrase from each column.

In a chemical reaction	the atoms	rearrange.
		reactants.
	energy	join together differently.
	the starting substances are	is transferred.
		products.

2. Sulfur dioxide reacts with oxygen to make sulfur trioxide. The diagram shows how the atoms rearrange and join together differently in the chemical reaction.

Sulfur dioxide...	...reacts with...	...oxygen ...	...to make...	...sulfur trioxide.
two SO₂ molecules		one oxygen molecule		two sulfur dioxide molecules

   a. Give the number of sulfur atoms shown in the reactants.

   b. Give the number of sulfur atoms shown in the products.

   c. Give the number of oxygen atoms shown in the reactants.

   d. Give the number of oxygen atoms shown in the products.

   e. In an experiment, 12.8 g of sulfur dioxide reacts with 3.2 g of oxygen. Predict the mass of sulfur trioxide made.

Extension

The diagram shows the reaction of methane with chlorine to make chloromethane and hydrogen chloride. Describe how the atoms rearrange and join together differently in the chemical reaction.

methane...   ...reacts with...   ...chlorine...   ...to make...   ... chloromethane...   ...and...   ...hydrogen chloride

1. Draw lines to match each word or symbol to its meaning.

Word or symbol		Meaning
reactants		reacts to make
products		the substances made in a chemical reaction
→		the starting substances in a chemical reaction

2. For the reactions below:
   - underline the names of the reactants
   - circle the names of the products

   a. Magnesium burns in oxygen to make magnesium oxide.

   b. When iron burns in oxygen, it makes iron oxide.

   c. Carbon and oxygen react together to make carbon dioxide.

   d. Sodium hydroxide neutralises hydrochloric acid to make sodium chloride and water.

   e. Hydrochloric acid and copper oxide react to make copper chloride and water.

3. Complete the word equations. Write the name of one substance on each line.

   a. zinc + oxygen → ....

   b. potassium + ... → potassium oxide

   c. carbon + ... → carbon dioxide

   d. .... + oxygen → sulfur dioxide

   e. silver nitrate + potassium iodide → silver iodide + ...

   f. calcium carbonate + sulfuric acid → calcium sulfate + ... + water

4. Write word equations for the combustion (burning) reactions of these elements.

   a. lithium ....

   b. calcium ....

   c. zinc ....

Extension

Write word equations to summarise the reactions below.

a. Heating calcium carbonate to make calcium oxide and carbon dioxide.

b. Reacting together aluminium and iodine to make aluminium iodide.

c. Reacting magnesium with sulfuric acid to make magnesium sulfate and hydrogen.

d. Reacting copper oxide and magnesium to make magnesium oxide and copper.

1. Make up four sentences using the phrases in the table. Each sentence must include a phrase from each column.

		the surroundings.
Exothermic changes	include	combustion reactions.
Endothermic changes	transfer energy to	freezing.
	transfer energy from	evaporating.

....

....

....

....

2. Highlight the correct word or phrases in each pair of **bold** words or phrases.

Parama holds an ice cube. The ice starts to **evaporate / melt**. Her hand feels **warm / cold**. This is because thermal energy is transferred **to / from** the hand. The energy makes the particles in ice **start / stop** moving around. Melting is **endothermic / exothermic.**

TWS 3. Vichit dissolves five substances (A, B, C, D, E) in water. He measures the water temperatures before dissolving and the solution temperature immediately after dissolving. His results are in the table.

Solute	Temperature of water before dissolving (°C)	Temperature of solution immediately after solute has dissolved (°C)	Temperature change (°C)
A	22	56	+34
B	24	72	
C	24	15	−9
D	23	10	
E	25	86	

a. Calculate the temperature changes for dissolving solutes B, D, and E. Write them in the table.

b. Give the letters of the changes that transfer thermal energy *to* the surroundings as the solutions return to room temperature. ....

c. Give the letter of the change that transfers the most thermal energy to the surroundings as the solution returns to room temperature. ....

d. Give the letters of the endothermic changes. ....

TWS e. Give the letters of the exothermic changes. ....

Extension

On a warm day, water evaporates from a pond. Explain why this process is endothermic.

Thinking and working scientifically

1. Zuberi investigates four fuels. He wants to find out which releases most energy when it burns. He sets up this apparatus.

   a. Complete the table to show the independent, dependent, and control variables.

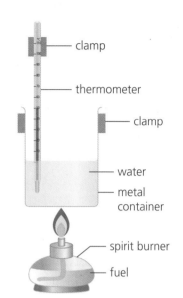

Variable	Independent, dependent, or control?
volume of water	
type of fuel	
mass of fuel burned	
temperature change of water	

   b. The table below summarises the results from the investigation.

Fuel	Temperature change (°C)			
	First time	**Second time**	**Third time**	**Average**
methanol	42	38	40	
ethanol	45	45	48	46
propanol	54	53	55	54
butanol	81	59	59	59

   i. Why did Zuberi repeat the test for each fuel three times?
      Tick the **two** best answers.

   To reduce error ☐
   To save fuel ☐
   To make the results more reliable ☐
   To make the water as hot as possible ☐

   ii. Highlight the anomalous result in the table.

   iii. Calculate the missing average and write it in the table.

   iv. Write a conclusion for the investigation.

   ....

   ....

Extension

Zuberi's teacher says that some of the thermal energy transferred by the fuel was not used to heat the water. Suggest what happened to this energy.

Extension

1. Cerena plans to compare the heat released when she burns three types of nut.
   She sets up the apparatus opposite.

   a. Name one piece of apparatus needed for the investigation that is not shown in the diagram.

   ....

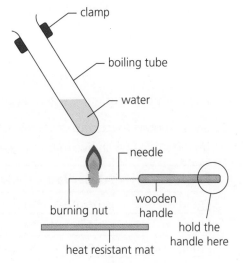

   b. The student lists some hazards for the investigation. Complete the table to show how she can reduce the chance of injury.

Hazard	Risk	Reduce chance of injury by...
hot apparatus and water	burns	
nuts	allergies	Do not do the experiment if someone in the class is allergic to nuts.

   c. The student repeats the test for each nut three times.

   i. Suggest why she repeats the test for each nut three times.

   ....

   ii. Draw a table for the results.

   d. The bar chart shows the results.
      List the nuts in order of increasing energy transferred on burning.

   ....

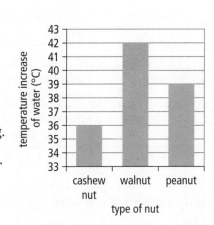

1. Use words and phrases from the box to complete the sentences. Use each word or phrase once, more than once, or not at all.

oxides	reactive	oxygen	iron oxide	chlorides

Some metals burn in air. They are reacting with .... from the air. The products of the

reactions are .... For example, iron filings burn in air to make ....

Magnesium burns more vigorously than iron. Magnesium is more .... than iron.

2. Some metals react with oxygen from the air without burning. The products are oxides. The table gives observations when five metals are exposed to air.

Metal	Observations when metal exposed to air
gold	The metal remains shiny for many years.
lithium	In 1 minute, the surface changes from shiny to dull grey.
magnesium	In a few weeks, the surface changes from shiny to dull grey.
potassium	In 1 second, the surface changes from shiny to dull grey.
sodium	In 20 seconds, the surface changes from shiny to dull grey.

   a. Name the metals in the table that react with oxygen without burning.

   ....

   b. List the metals in the table in order of reactivity, most reactive first.

   ....

3. Complete the word equations.

   a. magnesium + ... → magnesium oxide

   b. iron + oxygen → ....

   c. .... + oxygen → potassium oxide

   d. lead + oxygen → ....

   e. tin + ... → tin oxide

   f. .... + oxygen → zinc oxide

---

Extension

TWS Mrs Mangat heats a small piece of copper. She places the hot copper in a gas jar of oxygen. She repeats with three other metals. A student records his observations in a table.

Metal	Observations when hot metal placed in oxygen
copper	Gentle green flame. Surface becomes black.
iron	Orange flame and sparks. Surface becomes darker grey.
magnesium	Burns very vigorously with white sparks and a bright white flame. Makes white solid.
zinc	White and yellow sparks fly about. Makes yellow solid.

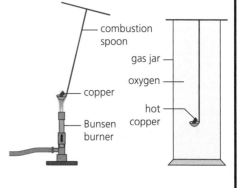

combustion spoon

gas jar

oxygen

copper

hot copper

Bunsen burner

TWS Explain what the observations in the table tell you about the order of reactivity of copper, iron, magnesium, and zinc.

1. Mr Fissoo plans to show his students how potassium reacts with water. His apparatus is below.

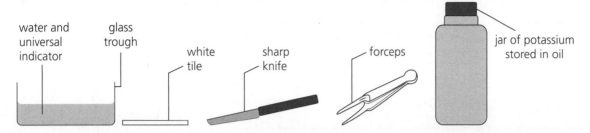

water and universal indicator   glass trough   white tile   sharp knife   forceps   jar of potassium stored in oil

a. The hazard symbols for potassium are shown below. Draw lines to match each hazard symbol with its meaning and one or more actions to reduce the chance of harm from the hazard.

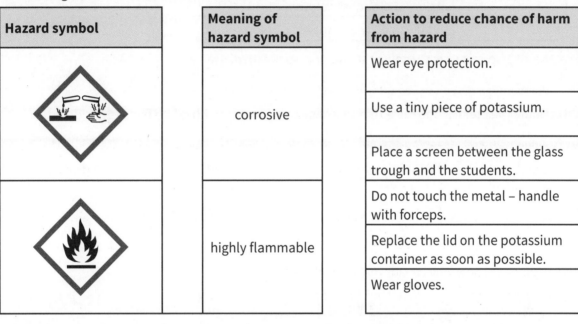

Hazard symbol	Meaning of hazard symbol	Action to reduce chance of harm from hazard
		Wear eye protection.
	corrosive	Use a tiny piece of potassium.
		Place a screen between the glass trough and the students.
		Do not touch the metal – handle with forceps.
	highly flammable	Replace the lid on the potassium container as soon as possible.
		Wear gloves.

b. A student writes down his observations. There is one mistake in each sentence. Highlight the mistakes and write the correction at the end of each line.

   • It was difficult to cut the potassium. ....
   • The potassium sank to the bottom of the water. ....
   • The potassium moved around slowly. ....
   • There was a yellow flame. ....
   • The universal indicator solution changed colour from green to red. ....

2. Write **T** next to the statements below that are true. Write **F** next to the statements that are false. Then write corrected versions of the **two** statements that are false.

a. When potassium reacts with water, one of the products is hydrogen gas.

b. Calcium reacts with water to make calcium hydroxide and oxygen gas.

c. Potassium reacts with water more vigorously than sodium and calcium react with water.

d. The word equation for the reaction of sodium with water is

   sodium + water $\rightarrow$ sodium hydroxide + oxygen

Corrected versions of false statements:

....

....

1. Sekani adds small pieces of different metals to dilute hydrochloric acid. He writes his observations in a table.

Metal	Observations when added to dilute hydrochloric acid
copper	no change
magnesium	bubbles vigorously and makes a colourless solution
gold	no change
zinc	bubbles less vigorously than magnesium and makes a colourless solution
iron	bubbles slowly and makes a green solution

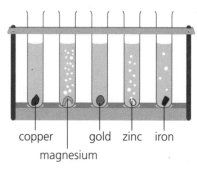

copper   gold   zinc   iron

magnesium

   a. Name two metals in the table that do not react with dilute hydrochloric acid.

   ....

   b. Name the metal in the table that reacts most vigorously with dilute hydrochloric acid.

   ....

   c. List the metals in the table in order of how vigorously they react with dilute hydrochloric acid. Write the most reactive metal first.

   ....

2. When metals react with dilute acids, the products are a salt and hydrogen gas.

   Draw lines to show which acids make which salts.

   a.

acid
hydrochloric
nitric
sulfuric

salts
sulfates
chlorides
nitrates

   b. Complete the word equations below.

   i.   magnesium + hydrochloric acid → magnesium chloride + ...

   ii. zinc + sulfuric acid → .... + hydrogen

   iii. iron + ... → iron chloride + ...

   iv. .... + hydrochloric acid → zinc chloride + ...

Extension

Eboni adds small pieces of magnesium ribbon to dilute hydrochloric acid in a beaker. The magnesium and acid react. Eboni stops adding magnesium when it no longer reacts.

Name the three substances in the beaker after Eboni has stopped adding the magnesium.

Use the reactivity series to the right to help you answer all the questions on this page.

1. For the metals in the reactivity series on this page:

   a. Name the most reactive metal. ....

   b. Name one inert metal. ....

   c. Name two metals that are more reactive than zinc. ....

   d. Name three metals that are less reactive than iron. ....

 2. Rehema compares the reactivity of iron, lead, and zinc. She adds samples of the metals to dilute hydrochloric acid.

| potassium |
| sodium |
| lithium |
| calcium |
| magnesium |
| zinc |
| iron |
| lead |
| copper |
| silver |
| gold |

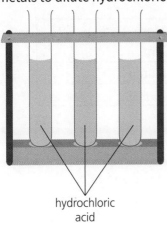

hydrochloric
acid

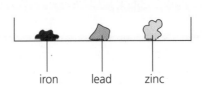

iron   lead   zinc

   a. Describe two things Rehema must do to compare the reactions fairly.

   ....

   b. Predict which of Rehema's metals will react most vigorously.

   ....

3. Mr Mathur compares the reactivity of zinc, iron, and copper. He sprinkles samples of the powdered metals into a Bunsen burner flame. He observes how vigorously the metals react with oxygen from the air.

   a. Predict the metal that will react least vigorously.

   ....

   b. Write a word equation for the reaction of zinc with oxygen.

   ....

4. Sakineh adds samples of metal to water. Draw lines to match each metal to the most likely observation.

metal
magnesium
calcium
copper

observation
no reaction
bubbles vigorously
small bubbles on surface of metal

Extension

Explain why attaching a piece of zinc or magnesium to a steel boat prevents the boat corroding. Remember, steel is mainly iron.

Thinking and working scientifically

The questions on this page are about another metal in the reactivity series – tin. A student compares the reactivity of tin with other metals (magnesium, copper, iron, lead and zinc) to find the position of tin in the reactivity series.

1. The student asks a question about tin

   Where is tin in the reactivity series?

   a. First, he adds a small piece of tin to hydrochloric acid. He compares his observations with the reactions of magnesium and copper.

Metal	Observations on adding to dilute hydrochloric acid
tin	bubbles slowly and makes colourless solution
magnesium	bubbles vigorously and makes colourless solution
copper	no change

   List the metals in the table in order of reactivity, most reactive first.

   ....

   b. Next, he compares the reactions of tin with three other metals (iron, lead, and zinc)

Metal	Observations on adding to dilute acid
iron	Bubbles slowly and makes a green solution.
lead	Bubble very slowly indeed to make a colourless solution.
tin	Bubbles slowly to make a colourless solution
zinc	Bubbles vigorously to make a colourless solution.

   i. State whether tin or zinc is more reactive. Explain your answer.

   ....

   ii. State whether tin or lead is more reactive. Explain your answer.

   ....

   iii. Write a conclusion to the investigation, based on the observations in question parts **a** and **b**.

   ....

   c. The student collects secondary data to compare the reactions of tin and iron with water.

   i. Suggest why he decides to compare the reactions of these two metals.

   ....

   ii. Suggest why the student decides to collect data from secondary sources, rather than by doing an experiment himself.

   ....

   iii. The table shows some of the student's data. Write a conclusion based on this data and the data in part **b**.

Metal	Reaction with water
iron	Reacts slowly with cold water in the presence of oxygen to make rust.
tin	Does not react with cold water. Reacts with steam to make tin oxide and hydrogen.

1. Write **T** next to the statements that are true. Write **F** next to the statements that are false. Then write corrected versions of the **two** false statements.

   a. Proton number is the number of protons in an atom.

   b. In the periodic table, the elements are arranged in order of mass number.

   c. The atomic number of an element is the same as its proton number.

   d. A helium atom has 2 protons and 2 neutrons, so its proton number is 4.

   Corrected versions of false statements:

   ....

   ....

2. The periodic table below shows the proton numbers of the elements.

1 hydrogen																	2 helium
3 lithium	4 beryllium											5 boron	6 carbon	7 nitrogen	8 oxygen	9 fluorine	10 neon
11 sodium	12 magnesium											13 aluminium	14 silicon	15 phosphorus	16 sulfur	17 chlorine	18 argon
19 potassium	20 calcium	21 scandium	22 titanium	23 vanadium	24 chromium	25 manganese	26 iron	27 cobalt	28 nickel	29 copper	30 zinc	31 gallium	32 germanium	33 arsenic	34 selenium	35 bromine	36 krypton
37 rubidium	38 strontium	39 yttrium	40 zirconium	41 niobium	42 molybdenum	43 technetium	44 ruthenium	45 rhodium	46 palladium	47 silver	48 cadmium	49 indium	50 tin	51 antimony	52 tellurium	53 iodine	54 xenon
55 caesium	56 barium	57–71 lanthanoids	72 hafnium	73 tantalum	74 tungsten	75 rhenium	76 osmium	77 iridium	78 platinum	79 gold	80 mercury	81 thallium	82 lead	83 bismuth	84 polonium	85 astatine	86 radon
87 francium	88 radium	89–103 actinoids	104 rutherfordium	105 dubnium	106 seaborgium	107 bohrium	108 hassium	109 meitnerium	110 darmstadtium	111 roentgenium	112 copernicium	113 nihonium	114 flerovium	115 moscovium	116 livermorium	117 tennessine	118 oganesson

   a. Give the proton numbers of these elements:

   i. arsenic ....   **iii.** silver ....

   ii. krypton ....

   b. Give the names of the elements with these proton numbers:

   i. 3 ....   **iii.** 13 ....

   ii. 7 ....   **iv.** 19 ....

   c. Predict the proton numbers of these elements:

   i. scandium ....   **iii.** tin ....

   ii. chlorine ....   **iv.** gold ....

3. A beryllium atom has 4 protons and 5 neutrons. Draw and label a diagram of the nucleus of the atom. Include a key.

   ┌─────────────────┐
   │   │
   │   │
   │   │
   │   │
   │   │
   │   │
   └─────────────────┘

Extension

Suggest why, in early periodic tables, the elements were arranged in order of atomic mass instead of in order of proton number.

10.2 Electrons in atoms

1. Highlight the correct **bold** words in the sentences below.

   The nucleus of an atom is made up of protons and **electrons / neutrons**. In a neutral atom, the number of electrons is equal to the number of **neutrons / protons**. The first electron shell holds a maximum of **2 / 8** electrons. The second electron shell holds a maximum of **2 / 8** electrons. The number and arrangement of electrons gives an element its **chemical / physical** properties.

2. Complete the table for the elements shown. For each element, the first number of the electron configuration is the number of electrons in the first shell. The second number is the number of electrons in the second shell, and so on.

Element	Number of electrons in one atom	Electron configuration
helium	2	
lithium		2,1
boron	5	
nitrogen	7	
fluorine	9	
magnesium		2,8,2
silicon	14	
sulfur	16	

3. Draw the electron configurations for the elements below.

lithium	beryllium	neon
sodium	magnesium	argon

Extension

Write the electron configurations for the first three elements in Group 1 (the left column) of the periodic table. Then compare the three electron configurations.

1. Choose words from the box to complete the sentences. Use each word once, more than once, or not at all.

| positively | ion | negatively | protons | electrons |

A particle with a positive or negative charge is called an .... An ion forms when an atom

gains or loses .... If an atom gains an electron, it becomes a .... charged ion.

If an atom loses an electron, it becomes a .... charged ion.

2. Complete the table for the ions shown.

Description of ion	Chemical formula of ion
A lithium ion, with a charge of +1	
A magnesium ion, with a charge of +2	
	Al^{3+}
A fluoride ion, with a charge of –1	F^-
A sulfide ion, with a charge of –2	
A nitride ion, with a charge of –3	

3. An atom or ion with a full outer shell is stable. Circle the electron configurations of the **two** stable atoms or ions below.

A   B   C   D

The diagram shows how ions are formed in the chemical reaction of sodium with chlorine.

Extension

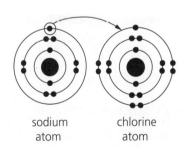

sodium atom   chlorine atom

a. Describe where the outer electron of a sodium atom moves from and to in the reaction.

b. Explain why the electron moves from one atom to another in the reaction.

c. Draw the electron configurations of the ions formed in the reaction.

1. Draw lines to match each phrase to its definition.

Phrase	Definition
ion	a substance that is made up of positive and negative ions
ionic bonding	the three-dimensional pattern of positive and negative ions
giant ionic structure	electrostatic attraction between positive and negative charges
ionic compound	a particle with a positive or negative charge

2. Most ionic compounds have similar physical properties. Highlight these properties in the list below.

   A. High melting point

   B. Low boiling point

   C. Brittle

   D. High boiling point

3. Some students explain why ionic compounds have high melting points. Write the name of the person who gives the **best** explanation.

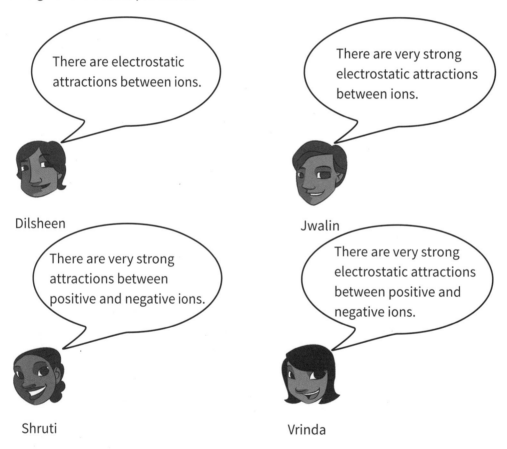

Dilsheen: There are electrostatic attractions between ions.

Jwalin: There are very strong electrostatic attractions between ions.

Shruti: There are very strong attractions between positive and negative ions.

Vrinda: There are very strong electrostatic attractions between positive and negative ions.

Name of person who gives the best explanation: ....

Extension

TWS Two students used grapes to make a physical model of ionic bonding.

Think of your own physical model of an ionic compound.

Draw a picture of your model, and label it.

TWS If possible, make your model.

1. Write **T** next to the statements that are true. Write **F** next to the statements that are false. Then write corrected versions of the **three** false statements.

   a. A covalent bond is a shared pair of electrons.

   b. Each covalent bond holds three atoms together.

   c. Compounds of metals have covalent bonds.

   d. Most non-metal elements exist as molecules.

   e. There is a covalent bond between the two atoms in a hydrogen molecule, H_2.

   f. There are four covalent bonds in an ammonia molecule, NH_3.

   Corrected versions of false statements:

   ....

   ....

   ....

2. A methane molecule is made up of carbon and hydrogen atoms. Diagrams **A** and **B** show the electron configurations of carbon and hydrogen. Diagram **C** shows how the electrons are shared in a methane molecule. The outer electron shells only are shown.

   Diagram **A** – carbon atom   Diagram **B** – hydrogen atom   Diagram **C** – methane molecule

   a. Complete the table by writing one number in each empty box of the table below.

Number of electrons in the outer shell of one carbon atom	
Number of electrons in the outer shell of one hydrogen atom	
Total number of electrons in the outer shell of the carbon atom in a methane molecule	
Total number of electrons in the outer shell of one hydrogen atom in a methane molecule	

   b. Explain why the carbon and hydrogen atoms in a methane molecule are stable.

   ....

Extension

Circle the two atoms that are most likely to form covalently bonded compounds.

A	B	C	D

1. The statements describe covalently bonded substances. Draw a tick (✓) in one box next to each statement to show the structure or structures it is true for.

Statement	True for substances with simple molecules	True for substances with giant covalent structures	True for simple molecules and giant structures
There are shared pairs of electrons between the atoms.			
The atoms are joined by covalent bonds.			
There is a three-dimensional network of atoms.			
The molecules are attracted to each other weakly.			
They have low melting points.			
Most are in the solid state at room temperature.			
They have high melting points.			
Most are in the gas or liquid state at room temperature.			

2. Write **M** next to the substances that exist as simple molecules. Write **G** next to the substances that have giant covalent structures.

   a. ammonia

   b. diamond

   c. hydrogen

   d. methane

   e. nitrogen

   f. silicon dioxide

3. Explain why a substance with a giant covalent structure has a higher melting point than a substance with simple molecules.

   ....

   ....

   ....

Extension

TWS The table shows the melting points of four substances.

Each substance is represented by a letter. The letters are not chemical symbols.

a. Predict the substances in the table that have simple molecules.

TWS **b.** Explain the choices you made in part **a**.

Substance	Melting point (°C)
W	−259
X	1710
Y	3550
Z	−182

1. Highlight the correct **bold** words and phrases in the sentences below.

   In a metal, each atom has lost one or more **electrons / protons**. This means that a metal structure has two types of particle – positively charged **electrons / ions** and negatively charged **electrons / ions**. The positively charged particles **do / do not** move. The negatively charged particles **do / do not** move. There are **covalent / electrostatic** attractions between the oppositely charged particles. The attractions are **strong / weak**. This means that a **large / small** amount of energy is needed to disrupt the structure, so metals have **high / low** melting points. A metal conducts electricity because its **electrons / ions** can move.

2. The diagram shows a metallic structure. Add a key to the diagram, to show what the two symbols mean.

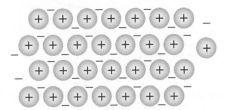

3. Draw lines to match each substance to its type of structure.

Substance
copper
sodium chloride
hydrogen sulfide
silicon dioxide

Type of structure
giant covalent
metallic
giant ionic
simple molecules

4. The table shows some properties of three substances.

   Each substance is represented by a letter. The letters are not chemical symbols. Complete the table with the structure each substance is most likely to have.

Substance	State at room temperature	Does it conduct electricity?	Type of structure. Choose from: • simple molecules • giant covalent • metallic
A	solid	yes	
B	gas	no	
C	solid	no	

Science in context

1. Some students give definitions of systematic reviews. Write the name of the person who gives the **best** definition.

> A systematic review identifies, compares, and evaluates primary evidence from different scientific papers to answer a scientific question.

Ameerah

> A systematic review uses secondary evidence to answer a scientific question.

Blessing

> A systematic review identifies and compares secondary evidence from different scientific papers.

Marcus

> A systematic review identifies, compares, and evaluates secondary evidence from different scientific papers to answer a scientific question.

Luther

Name of person who gives the best explanation: ....

2. A scientist might follow these steps when doing a systematic review.

   A. Make up a research question.

   B. Collect all the chosen data in one document.

   C. Tell other people about the paper at conferences and on social media.

   D. Decide which data to include, and which not to include.

   E. Make a conclusion.

   F. Find a scientific journal to publish the paper.

   G. Search for sources of data.

   H. Analyse the chosen data.

   I. Write a paper about the systematic review.

   Write the letters of the steps in a sensible order. The first has been done for you.

A								

3. When a scientist does a systematic review, they might not use all the available secondary data. Highlight **two** good reasons for this.

   A. Some papers might be in different languages.

   B. The scientist might think that some of the papers are more interesting than others.

   C. The scientist might judge that some of the research is not well done.

   D. The scientist might not like a scientist who did some of the research.

1. The steps below describe how to find the mass of some sand.

   A. Put the sand in the beaker.

   B. Do this calculation:

   mass of sand = (mass of beaker + sand) – mass of beaker

   C. Measure the mass of a beaker.

   D. Measure the mass of the sand and beaker together.

   Write the letters of the steps in the correct order. The first one has been done for you.

C			

2. Calculate the volumes of the blocks below.

   a.

   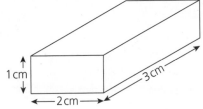

   ....
   ....

   b.

   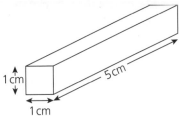

   ....
   ....

TWS 3. Use the diagrams to calculate the volume of the stone.

   Note: the diagrams show the lower parts of the measuring cylinders only.

   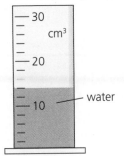 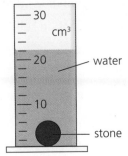

   ....
   ....

TWS

4. Mal-chin has samples of five materials, all in the solid state. He finds the mass and volume of each and writes the values in a table. Calculate the density of each material. Write your working and answers in the table.

Material	Mass (g)	Volume (cm³)	Working	Density (g/cm³)
balsa wood	16	8		
oak wood	42	6		
copper	38	2		
aluminium	2.7	1		

Extension

Calculate the mass of an iron cube of volume 4 cm³. The density of iron is 7.9 g/cm³.

1. Draw one line from each word to its definition.

Word		Definition
density		the amount of matter in an object
mass		the mass in a certain volume
volume		the amount of space an object takes up

2. The diagrams and labels show the density of four metal cubes.

zinc
density = 7.14 g/cm³

platinum
density = 21.4 g/cm³

tungsten
density = 19.4 g/cm³

iron
density = 7.86 g/cm³

Predict which of the four metals shown in the diagram has particles with the greatest mass.

....

3. The box gives some data for mercury.

Density of mercury in the liquid state at 20 °C = 13.6 g/cm³

Density of mercury in the solid state at 20 °C = 14.1 g/cm³

Highlight the one statement that best explains the density difference.

A. A particle of solid mercury has a greater mass than a particle of liquid mercury.

B. A particle of liquid mercury has a smaller mass than a particle of solid mercury.

C. The particles are less closely packed in liquid mercury than in solid mercury.

D. The particles are more closely packed in liquid mercury than in solid mercury.

Extension

TWS A student has some balls in a box. The balls are an analogy for the particle model.

Suggest how the student could use some of the balls – and the box – to explain why the density of a substance in the gas state is lower than its density in the solid state.

TWS

Science in context

1. Al-Biruni was a scientist and mathematician. He was born more than 1000 years ago.

   The table shows some things that al-Biruni did, and some things that scientists do today.

   Tick one or two boxes next to each action.

Action	Al-Biruni did this	Some or all scientists do this today
Ask scientific questions		
Do experiments		
Collect data		
Make conclusions		
Write about their work		
Publish their work on the internet		
Specialise in one area of science		
Study many areas of science		
Work in international teams		

2. The table gives the density values for some gemstones.

   Each gemstone has a range of density. For example, the density of diamond is between 3.50 and 3.53 g/cm^3.

Gemstone	Density (g/cm^3)
amber	1.05–1.09
diamond	3.50–3.53
garnet	3.78–3.85
lapis lazuli	2.50–3.00
opal	1.88–2.50
sapphire	3.95–4.03

   a. List the gemstones in order of increasing density, lowest density first.

   ....

   b. Gemstone X has a mass of 1.50 g and a volume of 1.40 cm^3.

   i. Calculate the density of the gemstone.
      Use this formula:

      $$density = \frac{mass}{volume}$$ ....

   ii. Suggest which of the gemstones in the table gemstone X is most likely to be ....

   iii. Suggest two other tests a scientist could do to confirm the identity of the gemstone.

   ....

   ....

Extension

Matteo has a diamond. Its mass is 0.30 g. Calculate the volume of the diamond. Assume that the density of the diamond is 3.50 g/cm3. Give your answer to two significant figures.

1. The list below describes some properties of elements.

   Write **M** next to the words and phrases that describe properties of most metals.
   Write **O** next to the words and phrases that describe properties of Group 1 metals.
   You will need to write both **M** and **O** next to some properties.
   Some of the properties in the list are not properties of any metals. Do not write on the lines next to these properties.

   a. shiny when freshly cut ....

   b. good conductor of electricity ....

   c. soft ....

   d. do not conduct electricity ....

   e. dull ....

   f. brittle ....

   g. melting point of 180 °C or lower...............................

TWS 2. The table gives the melting points and boiling points of the Group 1 elements.

Metal	Melting point (°C)	Boiling point (°C)
lithium	180	1330
sodium	98	890
potassium	64	774
rubidium	39	688
caesium	28	671

   a. i. Plot the **boiling point** data on the bar chart axes below.

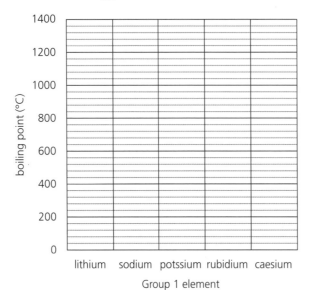

   ii. Describe the pattern on shown on your bar chart.

TWS

   ....

Extension

   a. Describe the pattern in **melting points** shown in the table.

   ....

   b. Explain the pattern in melting point shown in the table.

   ....

1. Shade in the Group 1 elements on the periodic table.

H																	He
Li	Be											B	C	N	O	F	Ne
Na	Mg											Al	Si	P	S	Cl	Ar
K	Ca	Sc	Ti	V	Cr	Mn	Fe	Co	Ni	Cu	Zn	Ga	Ge	As	Se	Br	Kr
Rb	Sr	Y	Zr	Nb	Mo	Tc	Ru	Rh	Pd	Ag	Cd	In	Sn	Sb	Te	I	Xe
Cs	Ba	La	Hf	Ta	W	Re	Os	Ir	Pt	Au	Hg	Tl	Pb	Bi	Po	At	Rn
Fr	Ra																

Note: This periodic table does not include all the elements.

2. Mr Okoro has samples of four different metals. He finds the mass and volume of each sample. His results are in the table.

Metal	Mass (g)	Volume (cm³)	Working	Density (g/cm³)
A	1.00	1.89		
B	3.00	0.14		
C	4.00	4.65		
D	2.00	0.10		

   a. Calculate the density of each metal. Use the equation density = $\dfrac{\text{mass}}{\text{volume}}$.

   Show your working and write your answers in the table.

   Give your answers to three significant figures.

   b. Write the letters of the metals that are most likely to be Group 1 elements.
   Explain your choices.

   ....

   ....

   ....

3. The Group 1 elements react vigorously with water.

   a. Complete the word equations for the reactions.

      i. lithium + water $\longrightarrow$ lithium .... + hydrogen

      ii. sodium + ... $\longrightarrow$ .... + hydrogen

      iii. potassium + ... $\longrightarrow$ .... + ...

   b. Describe the pattern in reactivity of the Group 1 elements with water.

   ....

   c. Explain the pattern in reactivity of the Group 1 elements with water.

   ....

   ....

1. Shade in the Group 2 elements on the periodic table.

H																	He
Li	Be											B	C	N	O	F	Ne
Na	Mg											Al	Si	P	S	Cl	Ar
K	Ca	Sc	Ti	V	Cr	Mn	Fe	Co	Ni	Cu	Zn	Ga	Ge	As	Se	Br	Kr
Rb	Sr	Y	Zr	Nb	Mo	Tc	Ru	Rh	Pd	Ag	Cd	In	Sn	Sb	Te	I	Xe
Cs	Ba	La	Hf	Ta	W	Re	Os	Ir	Pt	Au	Hg	Tl	Pb	Bi	Po	At	Rn
Fr	Ra																

Note: This periodic table does not include all the elements.

2. A scientist adds some Group 2 elements to water. She writes her observations in a table.

Group 2 element	Observations when added to cold water
Magnesium	Small bubbles form on surface of magnesium.
Calcium	Bubbles vigorously. Colourless solution formed.
Strontium	
Barium	Bubbles very vigorously indeed. Colourless solution formed.

a. Predict what the scientist will observe if she adds strontium to water.

....

b. When calcium reacts with water, the products are calcium hydroxide and hydrogen. Write a word equation for the reaction.

....

c. Write a word equation for the reaction of barium with water.

....

3. Magnesium reacts with hydrochloric acid to make magnesium chloride and water.

a. Predict the products of the reaction of calcium with hydrochloric acid.

....

b. Write a word equation for the reaction of calcium with hydrochloric acid.

....

Extension

TWS The table gives hardness values of some Group 1 and Group 2 elements. The bigger the value, the harder the element.

Element	Mohs hardness
lithium	0.6
sodium	0.5
potassium	0.4
rubidium	0.3
caesium	0.2

Element	Mohs hardness
beryllium	5.5
magnesium	2.5
calcium	1.5
strontium	1.5
barium	1.25

a. Plot the hardness values on two separate bar charts.

b. Describe the trend in hardness for the Group 2 elements.

TWS c. Compare the hardness values and trends for the Group 1 and Group 2 elements.

1. Write **T** next to the statements that are true. Write **F** next to the statements that are false. Then write corrected versions of the **three** sentences that are false.

   a. In a chemical reaction, there are more atoms in the products than in the reactants.

   b. In a chemical reaction, the mass of products is equal to the mass of reactants.

   c. In a chemical reaction, atoms rearrange and join together differently.

   d. In every chemical reaction, energy is transferred to the surroundings.

   e. In a chemical reaction, the starting substances are called products.

   f. In a chemical reaction, mass is conserved.

   g. In a chemical reaction, energy is conserved.

   Corrected versions of false statements:

   ....

   ....

   ....

2. Carbon monoxide reacts with oxygen to make carbon dioxide. The diagram shows how the atoms rearrange and join together differently in the chemical reaction.

   Carbon monoxide…   …reacts with…   …oxygen …   …to make…   …carbon dioxide.

   two CO molecules   one oxygen molecule   two CO_2 molecules

   a. Give the number of carbon atoms in the reactants.   ....

   b. Give the number of carbon atoms in the products.   ....

   c. Give the number of oxygen atoms in the reactants.   ....

   d. Give the number of oxygen atoms in the products.   ....

   e. Explain how your answers to parts **a–d** show why mass is conserved in this chemical reaction.

   ....

Extension

The symbol equation shows the reaction of sulfur dioxide and oxygen to make sulfur trioxide.

$2SO_2 + O_2 \longrightarrow 2SO_3$

a. Name the two reactants.

b. Name the product.

c. Give the meaning of the arrow in the chemical equation.

d. Write the formula of sulfur dioxide.

e. Write the formula of oxygen.

f. Write the formula of sulfur trioxide.

g. Give the number of sulfur trioxide molecules that are made when two SO_2 molecules react with oxygen.

h. Give the number of sulfur trioxide molecules that are made when 100 sulfur dioxide molecules react with oxygen molecules.

1. The balanced equation below shows the reaction of nitrogen with oxygen to make dinitrogen monoxide.

$$2N_2 + O_2 \longrightarrow 2N_2O$$

 a. Give the formula of an oxygen molecule. ....

 b. Give the formula of a dinitrogen monoxide molecule. ....

 c. Give the number of nitrogen atoms in one dinitrogen monoxide molecule. ....

 d. How many nitrogen molecules are shown in the equation? ....

 e. How many oxygen atoms are shown on each side of the equation? ....

2. Balance the equations below by writing balancing numbers where necessary. Do not change the formulae. A balancing number must be to the **left** of the formula it refers to. Some of the equations are already balanced.

 a. S + O_2 $\longrightarrow$ SO_2

 b. Zn + O_2 $\longrightarrow$ ZnO

 c. Mg + HCl $\longrightarrow$ $MgCl_2$ + H_2

 d. Zn + H_2SO_4 $\longrightarrow$ $ZnSO_4$ + H_2

 e. Na + H_2O $\longrightarrow$ $NaOH$ + H_2

 f. K + H_2O $\longrightarrow$ KOH + H_2

 g. Mg + CuO $\longrightarrow$ MgO + Cu

 h. $CuSO_4$ + Fe $\longrightarrow$ Cu + $FeSO_4$

3. Write balanced equations for the word equations below. Use the formulae in the box.

| C | O_2 | CO_2 | Mg | MgO | Zn | HCl | $ZnCl_2$ | H_2 | Li | H_2O | LiOH |
| $TiCl_4$ | | $MgCl_2$ | Ti | | | | | | | | |

 a. carbon + oxygen $\longrightarrow$ carbon dioxide

 ....

 b. magnesium + oxygen $\longrightarrow$ magnesium oxide

 ....

 c. zinc + hydrochloric acid $\longrightarrow$ zinc chloride + hydrogen

 ....

 d. lithium + water $\longrightarrow$ lithium hydroxide + hydrogen

 ....

 e. titanium chloride + magnesium $\longrightarrow$ magnesium chloride + titanium

 ....

1. Use the words and phrases in the box to complete the sentences below. Use each word or phrase once, more than once, or not at all.

less	displacement	copper sulfate	copper	more	displaces	iron sulfate	iron

Iron reacts with copper sulfate solution. The products are .... and ....
solution. This is a .... reaction. Iron is .... reactive than ....
The iron .... copper from its compound.

In general, a .... reactive metal displaces a .... reactive metal from its compounds in solution, and from its oxides.

2. Draw ticks in the boxes to show which pairs of metals and compounds react. Use the reactivity series on page **88** to help you. Do not tick the shaded boxes.

Metal \ Compound	magnesium chloride solution	iron chloride solution	lead nitrate solution	copper oxide
magnesium				
zinc				
iron				
lead				
copper				

3. Complete the word equations for the displacement reactions below.

   a. iron + copper sulfate solution ⟶ .... + ...

   b. magnesium + lead nitrate solution ⟶ .... + ...

   c. iron + copper oxide ⟶ .... + ...

   d. zinc + iron nitrate solution ⟶ .... + ...

   e. zinc + lead oxide ⟶ .... + ...

   f. magnesium + copper chloride solution ⟶ .... + ...

Extension

This question is about the thermite reaction.

   a. Name the two substances that react together in the reaction.

   b. Describe what you would see if you observed the reaction.

   c. Write a word equation for the reaction.

Science in context

1. Highlight the one correct word in each **bold** pair.

   The higher a metal is in the reactivity series, the **less / more** strongly its atoms are joined to atoms of other elements in its compounds. The more strongly the atoms are joined, the **less / more** difficult it is to extract the metal from its compounds. For example, zinc is **less / more** reactive than copper. It is **less / more** difficult to extract zinc from zinc oxide than it is to extract copper from copper oxide.

2. On the reactivity series opposite:

   a. Shade in one colour the metals that are extracted from their ores by electrolysis.

   b. Shade in another colour the metals that are extracted from their ores by heating with carbon.

   c. Leave unshaded the elements that are found in the Earth not joined to other elements.

potassium
sodium
lithium
calcium
magnesium
zinc
iron
lead
copper
silver
gold

3. Explain why some metals are extracted by heating their oxides with carbon, but some metals cannot be extracted in this way.

   ....

   ....

4. Complete the word equations below to show how the metals may be extracted from their oxides.

   a. tin oxide + carbon $\longrightarrow$ .... + ...

   b. lead oxide + carbon $\longrightarrow$ .... + ...

Extension

The list opposite shows the position of titanium in the reactivity series.

a. Suggest two metals that might extract titanium from its compounds.

b. Write word equations to show the reactions of these metals with titanium chloride.

sodium
magnesium
titanium
zinc
iron

Science in context

1. In the list below:
   a. Highlight in one colour the phrases that describe harmful environmental impacts of copper mining.
   b. Highlight in another colour reasons that explain why demand for copper is increasing.
   A. Copper mining results in many tonnes of waste rock.
   B. Copper wires join solar cells in solar farms.
   C. Land near copper mines cannot be used for farming.
   D. Lorries that move copper ore make greenhouse gases.
   E. Copper wires join wind turbines in wind farms.
   F. Machines that dig up copper ore make polluting gases and small solid particles.

2. Copper can be extracted from copper waste.
   a. Write three copper-containing things that people throw away.

   ....

   ....

   ....

   b. The steps below describe how copper can be extracted from copper waste.
      A. Spray sulfuric acid onto the waste.
      B. Add waste iron to the copper sulfate solution.
      C. This makes copper sulfate solution.
      D. This makes copper and iron sulfate.

   Write the steps in the best order. The first one has been done for you.

A			

   c. Complete the word equation for the reaction of copper sulfate solution with iron.

   copper sulfate + iron $\longrightarrow$ .... + ...

3. a. Write the name of the process in which plants are used to extract copper from copper ore

   waste. ....

   ....

   b. Write the name of the process in which new copper items are made by collecting and melting old

   copper items. ....

   ....

1. Four students say what they think a salt is.

Amit A salt is a substance that flavours food.

Baharupa A salt is a compound made from an acid.

Chandaka A salt is a compound made from an acid and a metal.

Dasbala A salt is a compound made when a metal ion replaces the hydrogen ion in an acid.

Write down the name of the person who gives the best definition of a salt. ....

TWS 2. A student plans to make zinc chloride from zinc and hydrochloric acid. She does a risk assessment. Draw lines to match each hazard and risk to show how to reduce the chance of injury from the risk.

Hazard and risk
dilute hydrochloric acid – corrosive
hydrogen gas – forms explosive mixture with air
hot equipment and solutions – burns
sharp edges of broken apparatus – cuts and damage to eyes

How to reduce chance of injury
wait for apparatus to cool before touching
wear eye protection and do not touch
keep away from flames
wear eye protection and inform teacher of breakages

TWS

3. The stages below describe how to make zinc chloride from a metal and an acid.

   A. Add zinc to hydrochloric acid until some unreacted solid zinc remains.

   B. Place the evaporating dish on a water bath.

   C. Leave in a warm place for a few days.

   D. Filter the mixture. Keep the solution.

   E. Heat the water bath until half the water has evaporated from the solution.

   F. Pour the solution into an evaporating basin.

   Write the letters of the stages in the correct order. The first one has been done for you.

A					

Extension

Suggest the metal and acid you could use to make calcium sulfate crystals.

12.7 More about salts

1. Write **T** next to the sentences that are true. Write **F** next to the sentences that are false. Then write corrected versions of the **three** sentences that are false.

   a. A salt is a compound made when a hydrogen ion replaces a metal ion in an acid.

   b. Nitric acid makes nitrate salts.

   c. Hydrochloric acid makes hydrochloride salts.

   d. Sulfuric acid makes sulfide salts.

   e. Chloride salts are formed when metals react with hydrochloric acid.

   f. Sulfates are formed when metals react with sulfuric acid.

   Corrected versions of false statements:

   ....

   ....

   ....

2. Name the salts made when these pairs of substances react together.

   a. Zinc and hydrochloric acid ....

   b. Magnesium and sulfuric acid ....

   c. Magnesium and hydrochloric acid ....

   d. Iron and sulfuric acid ....

   e. Magnesium and nitric acid ....

   f. Zinc and nitric acid ....

3. When metals react with acids, hydrogen gas is produced, as well as a salt. Describe how to test for hydrogen gas. Write down what you need to do, and what you would observe if hydrogen gas is present.

   ....

   ....

4. Complete the word equations.

   a. magnesium + hydrochloric acid $\longrightarrow$ .... + hydrogen

   b. zinc oxide + hydrochloric acid $\longrightarrow$ zinc chloride + ...

   c. copper carbonate + nitric acid $\longrightarrow$ copper .... + carbon dioxide + water

   d. nickel oxide + sulfuric acid $\longrightarrow$ nickel .... + ...

   e. magnesium + ... $\longrightarrow$ magnesium sulfate + ...

1. Complete the grid to predict the salts made when the substances in the grid react together. One has been done for you.

	Copper carbonate	Magnesium carbonate	Zinc carbonate
Hydrochloric acid			
Nitric acid		magnesium nitrate	
Sulfuric acid			

2. Copper carbonate reacts with hydrochloric acid to make a salt, water, and a substance that is a gas at room temperature.

   a. Name the salt that is made in the reaction. ....

   b. Name the substance formed in the reaction that is a gas at room temperature. ....

3. Complete the word equations below.

   a. copper carbonate + hydrochloric acid ⟶ .... + ... + water

   b. zinc carbonate + sulfuric acid ⟶ .... + carbon dioxide + ...

   c. magnesium carbonate + ... ⟶ magnesium nitrate + ... + ...

   d. .... + sulfuric acid ⟶ copper sulfate + carbon dioxide + ...

 4. Oona makes copper sulfate from copper carbonate and sulfuric acid. She follows the stages below.

   A. Add copper carbonate, a bit at a time, to 25 cm³ of dilute sulfuric acid. Stop adding copper carbonate when the reaction finishes.

   B. Filter the mixture. Keep the solution. Dispose of the solid.

   C. Pour the solution from stage B into an evaporating dish.

   D. Place the evaporating dish on a water bath.

   E. Heat the water bath until the volume of the solution is about half its original volume.

   F. Leave the remaining solution in a warm place for a few days.

   a. In stage **A**, how can Oona tell when the reaction finishes?

   ....

   b. Give the letters of three stages in which Oona is separating the components of mixtures.

   .... and .... and ....

   c. Give the letters of two stages that involve evaporation. .... and ....

> **Extension**
>
> Explain why it is better to heat the copper sulfate solution over a water bath rather than heating it directly.

1. Give an example of:

   a. A reaction chemists might want to slow down. ....

   b. A reaction chemists might want to speed up. ....

TWS **2.** Fatima follows the rate of the reaction between calcium carbonate and hydrochloric acid.

   a. Complete the word equation for the reaction.

   calcium carbonate + ... $\longrightarrow$ .... + carbon dioxide + water

   b. Fatima has a choice of two sets of apparatus.

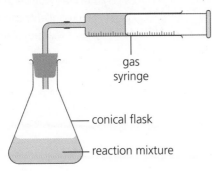

gas syringe

conical flask

reaction mixture

Apparatus A

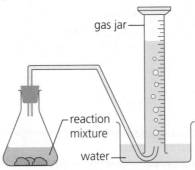

gas jar

reaction mixture

water

Apparatus B

Fatima's teacher says that apparatus B is not suitable for following this reaction. Tick the best reason for this from those below.

The gas made in the reaction (carbon dioxide) is not soluble in water. ☐

The gas made in the reaction (carbon dioxide) is soluble in water. ☐

The gas syringe measures smaller volume differences than the gas jar. ☐

The gas jar measures smaller volume differences than the gas syringe. ☐

   c. Fatima does the investigation and plots a graph.

   Fatima wants to label the graph. Her teacher gives her the labels below.

   Write **D** next to each label that **describes** part of the graph.

   Write **E** next to each label that **explains** part of the graph.

   i. The volume of gas is increasing quickly. ☐

   ii. The reaction is slowing down. ☐

   iii. The volume of gas is not changing. ☐

   iv. The volume of gas is increasing slowly. ☐

   v. The reaction is happening quickly. ☐

   vi. The reaction has finished. ☐

   d. Write the letters of the statements above in the correct boxes on the graph.

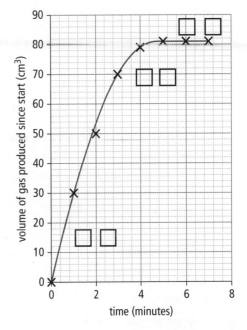

TWS

TWS **1.** Some students want to investigate how concentration affects reaction rate. They decide to investigate the reaction of zinc with sulfuric acid.

a. The students have some ideas about the investigation.

Harry I think that the more concentrated the acid, the faster the reaction.

Rebecca We can add zinc to sulfuric acid of different concentrations.

Louis The shorter the time for 1 g of zinc to be used up, the faster the reaction.

Flavia I wonder how acid concentration will affect reaction rate.

Give the name of a person who is:

i. asking a scientific question ....

ii. making a prediction ....

iii. suggesting how to collect evidence. ....

b. One student lists the variables in the investigation. Draw one tick (✓) next to each variable to show whether it is the independent variable, the dependent variable, or a control variable.

Variable	Independent variable	Dependent variable	Control variable
Concentration of acid			
Volume of acid			
Type of acid			
Time for zinc to finish reacting			
Size of zinc pieces			
Mass of zinc			

2. Which diagram represents the more concentrated acid solution?

● = acid particle

Not to scale. Water particles are not shown.

3. Use words from the box to complete the sentences. Use each word once, more than once, or not at all.

> more   slower   collide   less   faster

Substances react together when their particles .... The more concentrated an acid, the

.... frequently its particles .... with zinc particles, and the ....
the reaction.

Extension

Draw and label diagrams to explain why increasing the concentration of an acid increases the rate of reaction.

1. Some students want to investigate how temperature affects reaction rate. They decide to investigate the reaction of sodium thiosulfate solution with hydrochloric acid.

   a. The students discuss the investigation.

   Norbert I think that the hotter the solutions, the faster the reaction.

   Ebba At higher temperatures, particles move faster and collide more frequently. So at higher temperatures, the reaction will be faster.

   Wanda The higher the temperature, the more time is needed to finish the reaction.

   i. Give the name of the person who makes a hypothesis. ....

   ii. Give the name of the person who makes a prediction that is probably wrong. ....

   b. The students set up this apparatus. They measure the time for the cross to be hidden. Their results are in the table.

   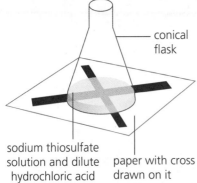

   conical flask

   sodium thiosulfate solution and dilute hydrochloric acid

   paper with cross drawn on it

Temperature (°C)	Time for cross to be hidden (s)
20	160
30	82
40	37
50	21
60	20
70	5

   i. The students decide to plot a line graph, not a bar chart. Explain why.

   ....

   ii. On graph paper, plot the results on a line graph.
   Label the *x*-axis *temperature (°C)*.
   Label the *y*-axis *time for cross to be hidden (s)*

   ....

   iii. On your graph, draw a circle around the anomalous result. Suggest why this result is anomalous.

   ....

   iv. A teacher tells the students to repeat their investigation twice more, and to calculate an average time for each temperature. Suggest why.

   ....

Extension

Look at your answer to question **a ii**. Use ideas about particles and collisions to explain why the prediction is probably wrong.

1. Circle the letter of the picture that shows the calcium carbonate with the greatest surface area.

A 1 g of calcium carbonate powder

B 1 g of small pieces of calcium carbonate

C 1 g of big pieces of calcium carbonate

 2. Kabira does an investigation to answer this question:

How does surface area affect the rate of reaction of calcium carbonate with hydrochloric acid?

She sets up this apparatus. She measures the time for the mass to decrease by 0.8 g for big pieces of calcium carbonate. She repeats for the small pieces and the powder.

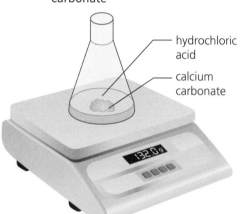

hydrochloric acid

calcium carbonate

a. Explain why the mass decreases. Use the word equation below to help you answer.

calcium carbonate + hydrochloric acid $\longrightarrow$
        calcium chloride + carbon dioxide + water

....

....

b. Kabira writes down her results.

The big pieces took 140 seconds and the powder was 30. The medium pieces went down by 0.8 g in 93 seconds.

i. Write Kabira's results in the table below.

Size of pieces	Time for mass to decrease by 0.8 g (s)

ii. Display Kabira's results on a bar chart.

iii. Write a conclusion for Kabira's investigation. Include a scientific explanation.

....

....

....

....

....

....

1. Write **T** next to the statements that are true. Write **F** next to the statements that are false. Then write corrected versions of the **three** false statements.

   a. A tectonic plate is a big slab of solid rock.

   b. There are about 32 tectonic plates.

   c. Tectonic plates move at speeds of a few centimetres/year.

   d. Natural processes deep in the Earth heat the mantle.

   e. There are conduction currents in the mantle.

   f. The moving of tectonic plates is called oceanic drift.

   Corrected versions of false statements:

   ....

   ....

   ....

2. The map shows the Earth's tectonic plates. The arrows show the direction of movement of the plates.

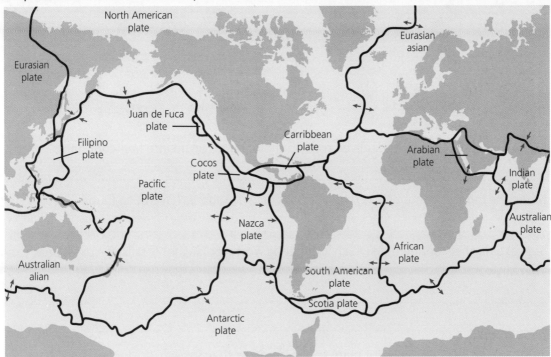

   a. State whether the Australian and Pacific plates are moving towards or away from each other.

   ....

   b. Name two plates that are moving away from each other.

   ....

   c. Explain why the distance between South America and Africa is increasing.

   ....

   d. Make up three questions about the tectonic plates map to ask to a friend.

   ....

   ....

   ....

1. The map shows areas where scientists have found fossils of the same species.

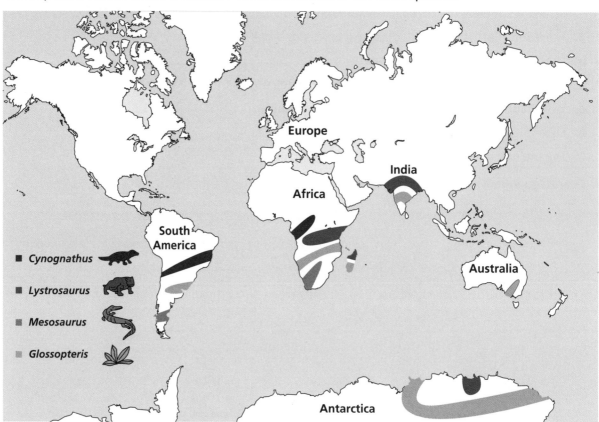

   a. Name one animal or plant that lived on land that later broke up into four continents.

   ....

   b. Name the modern continents on which fossils of *Cynognathus* have been found.

   ....

   c. Suggest another continent on which it might be worth looking for fossils of *Mesosaurus*. Explain
      your answer.

   ....

   ....

2. Describe two types of evidence for plate tectonics, other than fossils.

   ....

   ....

   ....

   ....

1. Draw one line from each phrase to its definition.

Phrase		Definition
tectonic plates		The movement of tectonic plates over millions of years.
continental drift		The approximately 12 slabs of solid rock that make up the Earth's crust and uppermost mantle.
seafloor spreading		A mountain chain on the sea floor.
oceanic ridge		The movement of the seafloor away from the two sides of an oceanic ridge.
earthquake		An opening in the Earth's crust that liquid rock and other materials escape from.
volcano		A sudden violent shaking of the ground.

2. The steps below describe how seafloor spreading happens.

    A. The convection currents make tectonic plates move.

    B. The magma cools and freezes.

    C. Processes deep in the Earth heat the mantle.

    D. Where plates move away from each other, magma rises through the gap.

    E. The heat drives convection currents in the mantle.

    Write the letters of the steps in the correct order. The first one has been done for you.

C				

3. Highlight the statement below that best describes evidence for seafloor spreading.

    A. The rock in oceanic ridges is rich in iron compounds.

    B. Convection currents in magma make some tectonic plates move away from each other.

    C. There are similar fossils on both sides of the Atlantic ocean.

    D. There is a symmetrical pattern of stripes in the rock on both sides of mid-ocean ridges.

Answers

1.1 The particle model

1. Materials, particles, mixtures, substances, sugar/silver, sugar/silver.

2. Particle separation – why 1 g of ice takes up less space than 1 g of steam; particle mass – why a gold coin is heavier than a silver coin of the same mass; if and how the particles move – why liquid water flows but solid rock does not flow; how strongly the particles hold together – why gold is easier to scratch than diamond.

Extension

Substances only – **B**, **C**.
Materials and substances – **A**, **D**, **E**.

1.2 The states of matter

1. Three, gas, gas, liquid, gas.

2. **a.** Particles arranged in rows, touching their neighbours.

   b. Vibrate on the spot.

3. Particles should touch their neighbours and the bottom of the container.

4. All – **A**.
   Gases and liquids – **C**, **F**, **G**.
   Solids and liquids – **D**, **E**.
   Gases only – **B**.
   Solids only – **H**, **I**.

Extension

a. R – the particles move around, sliding over each other all the time, so you can pour a liquid.

b. Q – the particles are always touching each other, so a given mass of liquid cannot get bigger (assuming the temperature does not change).

1.3 Using the particle model

1. **a.** For example, keeping vaccines cold.

   b. For example, in oxygen cylinders for fire fighters.

   c. For example, drinking, washing.

2. **B**

3. A substance flows in the liquid and gas states – the particles move around.
   A substance can be compressed only a tiny bit in the solid and liquid states – the particles touch each other.
   The shape of a substance in the liquid or gas state depends on the container it is in – the particles move around.
   A substance can be compressed a lot in the gas state – the particles are far apart.

Extension

a. For example, if a gas has a smell, you can smell it quickly across a room.

b. For example, if you put a powder on the surface of liquid water and observe through a microscope, the pieces of powder move around.

c. For example, the shape of a substance does not change in the solid state.

d. For example, if you melt a block of ice and then heat the liquid water until it has all evaporated, the steam takes up more space than the ice.

1.4 Changes of state – evaporating, boiling, and condensing

1. True – **b**, **d**.
   False – **a**, **c**.

   Corrected false statements:
   a. Condensing is the change of state from gas to liquid.

   c. When a substance changes state from liquid to gas, its particles get further apart.

2. **a.** D

   b. B

3.

	True of evaporation only	True of boiling only	True of both evaporation and boiling
This involves a change of state from a substance in its liquid state.			✓
Particles leave the surface of the liquid only.	✓		
Bubbles of the substance in its gas state form throughout the liquid.		✓	
This can happen at any temperature.	✓		
During this change of state, the particles get further apart.			✓

Extension

a. Methane.

b. Ethane, methane.

c. Hexadecane.

1.5 Investigating boiling points

1. Hypothesis – a possible explanation that is based on evidence and that can be tested further; anomalous result – a piece of data that does not fit the pattern in a series of results; conclusion – a description of what an experiment shows, with an explanation.

2. a.
   - Pour a known volume of water into a beaker, place on a tripod and gauze, heat with a Bunsen burner, use the thermometer to measure the boiling temperature, record the temperature in a table.
   - Get a fresh beaker of the same volume of water, add one spoonful of salt, stir until the water dissolves, repeat the step above
   - Repeat the first two steps above with 3, 4, and 5 spoonfuls of salt.
   - Plot a graph of the results.
   - Look at the graph – if the boiling temperature increases as the amount of salt increases, her hypothesis is correct.

   b. i. Data plotted correctly.

   ii. Point at (3, 101).

iii. As amount of salt increases, boiling temperature increases.

iv. For example, use a balance to measure mass of salt.

1.6 Changes of state – melting and freezing

1. Solid, liquid, move out of, move around, touch each other, strongly.

2. a. Sodium.

   b. Sodium, lead, copper, manganese, iron, chromium.

   c. Copper.

Extension

a. i. water; ii. mercury

b. Horizontal scale from approximately −120 °C to +360 °C, with divisions evenly spaced.

c. Melting points and boiling points correctly plotted on the scale, all labelled with name of substance and whether it is a melting point or boiling point.

d. i. gas
   ii. liquid
   iii. mercury

1.7 Models in science

1. **D**

2.

	This is a strength of the particle model	This is a limitation of the particle model	This can be a strength or a limitation
The particle model explains why some properties of a substance are different in the liquid and gas states.	✓		
In the particle model, each particle is a sphere.		✓	
The particle model cannot explain all properties.		✓	
The particle model explains why different substances have different melting points.	✓		
Some predictions made with the particle model are not correct.		✓	
The particle model is simpler than reality.			✓

3. For example:

   Better – tomato model 3D; can move tomatoes to represent changing movement and positions of particles in changes of state.

   Worse – difficult to arrange tomatoes in regular pattern to represent solid state; difficult to hold tomatoes in positions far apart to represent particles in gas state.

2.1 Elements and the periodic table

1. True – **a**, **d**.
   False – **b**, **c**, **e**.
   Correct versions of false statements:
   b. An element cannot be split up to make other substances.
   c. There are about 100 elements
   e. In the periodic table, metals are on the left of the stepped line.

2. Elements – gold, copper, vanadium, iodine, oxygen, chlorine.

3. Metals – lithium, manganese, nickel, rhodium, tungsten, vanadium, yttrium, zirconium.
   Non-metals – oxygen, phosphorus, sulfur, xenon.

4. a. Hydrogen, helium.
   b. Nitrogen.
   c. Carbon.
   d. Silver.
   e. Iron.

Extension

Answer depends on elements chosen.

2.2 Discovering the elements

1. a. i. Three from – copper, silver, gold, iron, tin, lead, carbon, sulfur.
      ii. Because they exist naturally on their own.
   b. i. hydrogen, nitrogen, oxygen, chlorine.
      ii. They are reactive and form stable compounds, which couldn't be broken up until 1700s.

Extension

a. No other known element had the same properties.

c. Difficult to communicate over great distances in the early 1800s.

d. Different samples of cast iron had different properties.

2.3 Chemical symbols

1. a. Mg
   b. Be
   c. Fe

2.

Name of element	chemical symbol
hydrogen	H
helium	He
lithium	Li
beryllium	Be
boron	B

carbon	C
nitrogen	N
oxygen	O
fluorine	F
neon	Ne

3.

Chemical symbol	Name of element
Na	sodium
Mg	magnesium
Al	aluminium
Si	silicon
P	phosphorus
S	sulfur
Cl	chlorine
Ar	argon
K	potassium
Ca	calcium

4. Re V I Si O N I S Ne Ce S S Ar Y – revision is necessary.

Extension

a. P
b. Cl
c. Be

2.4 Atoms

1. True– **a, c, e, f**.
   False– **b, d, g**.
   Corrected versions of false statements:

   b. A model is an idea that explains observations and helps in making predictions.

   d. One copper atom on its own does not have the same properties as a block of copper.

   g. Platinum and silver atoms are different.

2. a. B, C, D, F
   b. A, E
   c. C, D
   d. B, F
   e. C, D

Extension

10 000 000 000 000

2.5 Organising the elements

1. Top – Dalton; second row – Cannizzaro; third row – Mendeleev; fourth row, from left – French, Swedish, Tacke/Noddack, Tacke/Noddack.

Extension

a. To see if its properties matched those predicted by Mendeleev.

b. Gave them confidence that the periodic table was correct.

2.6 Compounds

1. Two, strongly, different, two, strongly.

2. Hydrogen – gas, burns easily; oxygen – element; water – compound, liquid, puts out fires.

3. a. An idea that explains observations and helps in making predictions.

   b. Strengths – 3D, making it easier to picture molecules; shows arrangements of atoms in molecules; atoms of different elements easy to distinguish because they are different sizes and colours.

   Weaknesses – not easily transportable; expensive; waste of food.

Extension

a. A, C

b. A, D

c. C

d. D

2.7 What's in a name?

1. a. Magnesium oxide.

   b. Iron sulfide.

   c. Aluminium chloride.

   d. Iron bromide.

   e. Potassium iodide.

   f. Sodium nitride.

2. a. Calcium, carbon, oxygen.

   b. Iron, sulfur, oxygen.

   c. Sodium, nitrogen, oxygen.

   d. Potassium, phosphorus, oxygen.

3. a. Sodium carbonate.

   b. Magnesium nitrate.

   c. Copper sulfate.

4.

Molecule of compound made up of...	Name of compound
1 atom of carbon and 2 atoms of oxygen	carbon dioxide
1 atom of carbon and 1 atom of oxygen	carbon monoxide
1 atom of nitrogen and 2 atoms of oxygen	nitrogen dioxide
1 atom of sulfur and 3 atoms of oxygen	sulfur trioxide
1 atom of sulfur and 2 atoms of oxygen	sulfur dioxide

Extension

a. Carbon dioxide.

b. Carbon monoxide.

c. Sulfur trioxide.

2.8 Chemical formulae

1. a. 2, 1

   b. 2

   c. 2, 1

2. Iodine – I_2; dinitrogen tetroxide – N_2O_4; carbon monoxide – CO; carbon dioxide – CO_2; sulfur trioxide – SO_3.

3. a. H_2O

   b. CO_2

   c. O_2

4. Potassium iodide – KI; lithium oxide – Li_2O; sodium nitrate – $NaNO_3$; calcium sulfate – $CaSO_4$; magnesium carbonate – $MgCO_3$.

a. 13 carbon atoms, 12 hydrogen atoms, 1 nitrogen atom, 3 oxygen atoms.

b. $13 \times 5 = 65$ carbon atoms; $12 \times 5 = 60$ hydrogen atoms; $1 \times 5 = 5$ nitrogen atom; $3 \times 5 = 15$ oxygen atoms.

2.9 What's in a mixture?

1. True – **c**, **e**.
   False – **a**, **b**, **d**.

   Corrected versions of false statements:
   a. The different substances in a mixture are not joined together.
   b. You can change the amounts of substances in a mixture.
   d. In a mixture, the substances keep their own properties.

2.

Mixture	Mixture of elements only	Mixture of compounds only	Mixture of element(s) and compound
nitrogen and oxygen	✓		
sodium chloride (salt) dissolved in water		✓	
chlorine dissolved in water			✓
nitrogen, oxygen, and carbon dioxide			✓

3. a. B
   b. C
   c. A
   d. D
   e. E

Extension

Mixture of elements and compounds.

2.10 What's in a solution?

1. Solute – a substance that dissolves in a liquid to make a solution;
   solvent – the liquid that a substance dissolves in;
   solution – a mixture made when a substance dissolves in a liquid;
   dissolving – the processes of adding a solid to a liquid so that you can no longer see separate pieces of solid;
   soluble – able to dissolve;
   insoluble – when a substance cannot mix with a liquid to make a solution.

2. A – sugar particles are randomly positioned and mixed with and surrounded by water particles.

3. $250\ g + 10\ g = 260\ g$

Extension

Name	Correct or incorrect?
Kamol	correct
Lawan	incorrect – the solution is a mixture of two compounds
Mongkut	correct
Niran	incorrect – copper sulfate is soluble in water
Pakpao	incorrect – copper sulfate is the solute and water is the solvent
Ratana	correct

2.11 Comparing elements, mixtures, and compounds

1. An element, cannot, element, compound, different.

2.

	Mixtures of elements	Compounds
Can it easily be separated into its elements?	yes	no

	Mixtures of elements	Compounds
How do its properties compare to those of its elements?	similar	not similar
Are its elements joined together?	no	yes
Can you change the amounts of each element in 100 g of the mixture or compound?	yes	no

3. **a.** E

   b. B

   c. A

   d. C

   e. D

Extension

Paragraph covering the points in the table in question **2**.

2.12 What are you made of?

1. Carbon, hydrogen, oxygen, nitrogen.

2. Hydrogen, oxygen.

3. **a.** Keratin.

   b. Carbon, hydrogen, oxygen, nitrogen, sulfur.

4. **a.** 2.3 g

   b. For example, meat, beans, lentils, green vegetables.

   c. In haemoglobin, to carry blood around the body.

   d. Tiredness, dizziness, weakness.

Extension

Paragraph covering the information in the table on Student Book page 59.

3.1 Magnificent metals

1. Sonorous, shiny when freshly cut, high melting point, good conductor of thermal energy, strong, ductile, good conductor of electricity, hard, malleable.

2. Heat sink – good conductor of thermal energy; bells – sonorous; bicycle frames – strong and malleable; electric cables – good conductor or electricity; cooking pans – good conductor of thermal energy; coins – shiny; printed circuit boards – good conductor of electricity.

Extension

a. Lithium, sodium, and potassium have lower melting points than other metals, for example, copper, gold, and silver.

b. Similar – shiny when you first cut them, good conductors of electricity; different – soft, low melting point.

3.2 Comparing conductors

1. **a.** Independent – material the spoon is made of; dependent – time for butter to melt; control – size of spoon, amount of butter, temperature of water, distance from water to butter.

   b. The spoons are different sizes.

   c. The butter on the silver spoon melts quickest, showing that silver is the best conductor of thermal energy. The butter on the plastic spoon melts slowest, showing that plastic is the worst conductor of heat.

Extension

a. The metal elements in the table have higher thermal conductivity values, so are better conductors of thermal energy than non-metals.

b. Any suitable answer, for example: no, because carbon could just be a single exception; yes, because carbon is a non-metal and its thermal conductivity value is high, suggesting that it is not only metals that are good conductors of heat.

3.3 Amazing alloys

1. True– **b**, **c**, **f**.
   False– **a**, **d**, **e**.

   Corrected versions of false statements:

   a. An alloy is a mixture of a metal with small amounts of other elements.

   d. Most alloys are stronger than the elements that are in them.

   e. Most alloys are harder than the elements that are in them.

2. **a.** In pure iron, the atoms are arranged in straight rows. In steel, the straight rows are disrupted by the presence of smaller, randomly placed carbon atoms.

   b. The iron atom layers cannot slide over each other easily in steel, but they can slide over each other easily in pure iron.

Extension

a. Differences – the alloy is almost five times harder than pure titanium, the alloy is about four times stronger than pure titanium; similarities – both are shiny and both are not damaged when exposed to air or water.

b. The alloy is stronger because the different-sized aluminium and vanadium atoms disrupt the layers of titanium atoms, meaning that the layers of atoms can no longer slide over each other easily.

3.4 Non-metal elements

1. Brittle, poor conductor of thermal energy, low melting point, poor conductor of electricity, dull.

2. C, E

3. **a.** I, L, K, J, G, H

   b. G, H, J

Extension

a. Shiny, conducts electricity.

b. Brittle.

c. Yes, because two of the properties given are typical of metals and one is typical of non-metals.

3.5 Explaining properties of metals and non-metals

1. Elements on right of stepped line coloured in.

2. **a.** Their atoms are held together strongly.

   b. Their atoms are held together strongly.

3. **a.** It exists as molecules, which are attracted to each other only weakly.

   b. If a crystal drops, it breaks between rows of molecules.

Extension

Metals – J, L, M because their thermal conductivity values are much higher than those of the other elements in the table.

3.6 Better bicycles

1. Low density, stiff, hard, shiny, strong, not damaged by air and water.

2. **a.** B

   b. Because it has the lowest density, and is hardest. It is also stiff and strong.

   c. It is renewable / can be obtained with minimal damage to the environment.

Extension

Any appropriate answer.

4.1 What are chemical reactions?

1. Substances, rearrange, differently, reverse, energy, reactants, products.

2.

Description of reaction	Reactant name(s)	Product name(s)
Magnesium reacts with oxygen to make magnesium oxide.	magnesium oxygen	magnesium oxide
Iron reacts with sulfur to make iron sulfide.	iron sulfur	iron sulfide
Magnesium reacts with hydrochloric acid to make magnesium chloride and hydrogen.	magnesium hydrochloric acid	magnesium chloride hydrogen
Sodium hydroxide reacts with copper sulfate to make copper hydroxide and sodium sulfate.	sodium hydroxide copper sulfate	copper hydroxide sodium sulfate
On heating, copper carbonate makes copper oxide and carbon dioxide.	copper carbonate	copper oxide carbon dioxide

3. a. Flammable.

b. Keep it away from flames.

Extension

Magnesium has magnesium atoms only; magnesium oxide has both magnesium atoms and oxygen atoms (from the air).

4.2 Atoms in chemical reactions

1. True– **a, c, d.**

False– **b, e.**

Corrected versions of false statements:

b. In a chemical reaction, the total mass of products is equal to the total mass of reactants

e. A water molecule has two hydrogen atoms joined to one oxygen atom.

2. a. 2

b. 2

c. 2

d. 2

e. The number of atoms of each element is the same in the reactants and products.

Extension

Reactants – 1 methane molecule (1 carbon atom joined to 4 hydrogen atoms) and 2 oxygen molecules (2 oxygen atoms in each); products – 1 carbon dioxide molecule (1 carbon atom joined to 2 oxygen atoms) and 2 water molecules (each with 1 oxygen atom joined to 2 hydrogen atoms).

4.3 Investigating a chemical reaction

1. From top – hypothesis, prediction, conclusion.

2. a. 27 g – 25 g = 2 g

b. Colour change from green solid to black solid.

c. One of the products, carbon dioxide, leaves the test tube as a gas as it is made.

d. 26 g – 25 g = 1 g

e. 2 g – 1 g = 1 g

f. The mass of solid product is less than the mass of solid reactant because one of the products (carbon dioxide) forms as a gas that leaves the test tube.

4.4 Precipitation reactions

1. Soluble substance – a substance that dissolves in a solvent;
   insoluble substance – a substance that does not dissolve in a solvent;
   precipitate – a suspension of tiny solid particles in a liquid or solution;
   precipitation reaction – a reason in which two substances react to make a precipitate;
   combustion reaction – a reaction in which a substance reacts quickly with oxygen.

2. **a.** Lead iodide.

   b. Copper hydroxide.

3. Copper.

4. From top – oxidising/makes other substances burn easily; hazard to health; corrosive/burns skin and eyes; danger to environment.

4.5 Corrosion reactions

1. On the surface of, damage, slowly, oxygen, rust, exposes, can.

2. Physical properties – for example, melting point, properties you can observe or measure without changing a substance;
   chemical properties – how the substance takes part in chemical reactions, for example, how quickly a substance corrodes or if it burns, you can only find out about these by doing chemical reactions.

3. Oil or grease – stops air and water touching surface;
   alloy – does not react with oxygen at all;
   painting – stops air and water touching surface;
   covering with zinc – stops air and water touching surface.

5.1 Acids and alkalis

1. Acidic substances, for example – lemons, limes, vomit;
   alkaline substances, for example – toothpaste, soap.

2. **a.** Corrosive – hazard symbol showing drips onto hand and flat surface.
   Reduce risks by wearing eye protection and gloves.

3. Acidic; reason – indicator becomes the same colour as its colour in hydrochloric acid.

5.2 The pH scale

1. True– **a**, **d**, **f**.
   False– **b**, **c**, **e**.
   Corrected versions of false statements:
   b. An alkaline solution has a pH greater than 7.0.
   c. The more acidic a solution, the lower its pH.
   e. You can use litmus paper to find out whether a solution is acidic or alkaline/you can use universal indicator to find out the pH of a solution.

2. **a.** Making fertilisers.

   b. 2%

5.3 Neutralisation reactions

1. True– **a, e, f**.
   False– **b, c, d**.
   Corrected versions of false statements:
   b. If you add water to an acid, its concentration decreases;
   c. Alex has an alkali of pH 12. He adds acid. The pH decreases;
   d. If your soil is too acidic for a certain crop, add alkali to the soil to increase its pH

2. Purple, alkaline, decreases, 7, neutralised, decreases, red.

Extension

C

5.4 Investigating neutralisation

1. **a.** It is possible to answer this question by finding the mass of limestone needed to increase the pH of a sample of water to pH 7.0, and then to scale up to find the mass needed for all the water in the pond.

   b. i. Mass of limestone
   ii. pH after adding limestone
   iii. So that the test is fair

   c. i. 20 g, this is the minimum amount of limestone required to achieve a neutral pH.
   ii. The volume/amount of water in the pond.

5.5 Acid rain

1. **a.** Cause.
   b. Effect.
   c. Cause.
   d. Effect.
   e. Effect.
   f. Cause.
   g. Cause.

2. **a.** Nitric acid, calcium carbonate.
   b. Calcium nitrate, water, carbon dioxide.

Extension

Any sensible suggestions.

5.6 Gas products of acid reactions

1. **a.** Carbon dioxide: CO_2, limewater, goes milky.
   b. Oxygen: O_2, glowing splint, splint relights.
   c. Hydrogen: H_2, lighted splint, flame goes out with a squeaky pop.

2.

Reaction	Names of reactants	Names of products
A	hydrochloric acid calcium carbonate	calcium chloride water carbon dioxide
B	zinc hydrochloric acid	zinc chloride hydrogen

Extension

Any correct properties and uses.

6.1 Models of the Earth

1. From top – crust, mantle, outer core, inner core.

2. **a.** I
   b. C, M, I
   c. O
   d. O, I
   e. M, O
   f. C
   g. C

3. Ships appear to sink as they go over the horizon, observations from space, the shadow of the Earth on the Moon is round.

Answers

6.2 Plate tectonics

1. Evidence for plate tectonics – scientists found fossils of the same animal in Africa and South America; scientists found fossils of the same plants in Africa and South America; shapes of Africa and South America look as if they fit together.
   Reasons that other scientists rejected the idea of plate tectonics at first – scientists did not know *how* the continents could move; scientists did not trust Wegener (the scientist who suggested the hypothesis) because he mainly studied the weather, not rocks.

2. Methods that could not have been used 50 years ago – text message, email, shared web pages.

Extension

Expeditions – Greenland; continental drift – suggested continents had once been joined together and are now moving apart; interesting things about his life – anything suitable.

6.3 The restless Earth

1. A, G, E, H, B, D, I, F, C

2. Nazca and South American plate moved towards each other, they collided and the edges of the continents crumpled together and piled up to make the Andes mountains.

Extension

a. B, C
b. A, D

6.4 Volcanoes

1. True– **a, b, c, f**.
   False– **d, e, g**.
   Corrected versions of false statements:
   d. Lava is liquid rock that is on the surface of the Earth;
   e. Magma is liquid rock that is under the ground;
   g. There are about 500 active volcanoes in the world.

2. When the steepness of a volcano slope changes, the volcano may erupt – this change may be caused by magma pushing up against surface rock.

   When there are more earth movements near a volcano, the volcano may erupt – This change may be caused by magma moving inside the volcano.

   Magma often contains dissolved sulfur dioxide. When extra sulfur dioxide gas comes out of a volcano, the volcano may erupt – this change may be caused by magma moving upwards.

   When the surface temperature of a volcano changes, the volcano may erupt – this change may be caused by magma pushing up against surface rock.

Extension

a. Lisimba.
b. Muna.
c. Kibibi.

7.1 Inside atoms

1.

Phenomenon	The solid sphere model of atoms *can* explain this.	The solid sphere model of atoms *cannot* explain this.
condensing	✓	
chemical reactions		✓
melting	✓	

2. Left – nucleus; right, from top – electron, proton, neutron.

3. a. 5

   b. 19

   c. 28

   d. 33

4. Carbon – diagram showing 6 protons and 6 neutrons; beryllium – diagram showing 4 protons and 5 neutrons; fluorine – diagram showing 9 protons and 10 neutrons.

> **Extension**
>
> Like an atom – similar shape, includes small electrons/pips; unlike an atom – no nucleus, no parts represent protons and neutrons; overall usefulness – any well-argued answer.

7.2 Discovering electrons

1. Scientific question – what are cathode rays? Hypothesis – cathode rays move towards a positive electrode, so they might have a negative electrical charge.
Prediction – if I pass cathode rays between electrically charged pieces of metal, the rays will change direction. The rays will bend towards the positively-charged metal.
Conclusion – cathode rays are charged. Their charge is negative.

2. a. Both include separate positive and negative charges, both state that atoms are spherical.

   b. Thomson – electrons are placed throughout the sphere; Nagaoka – electrons orbit outside the centre of the atom in rings.

> **Extension**
>
> Like Thomson's model – electrons spread throughout melon, no nucleus; unlike Thomson's model – has a tough skin; overall usefulness – any well-argued answer.

7.3 Finding the nucleus

1. a. A, B, C, F

   b. D, E

   c. G

2. Most particles travel straight through the foil – these particles travel through the empty space between nuclei.
A very few particles bounce backwards off the foil – these particles hit a positively charged nucleus.
Some particles change direction a little as they travel through the foil – these particles travel close to a positively charged nucleus.

> **Extension**
>
> 1803 – **A**, 1800s – **E**, 1904 – **F**, 1909 – **B**, 1911 – **C**, 1913 – **D**, 1932 – **G**.

7.4 Inside sub-atomic particles

1. a. Suggested that there is a particle (Higgs boson) that gives protons and neutrons their mass. Described properties of the Higgs boson. – Use creative thought to make a hypothesis.
Built the Large Hadron Collider and made protons collide in it. Observed the products of the collisions. – Collect evidence.
Wondered what gives protons and neutrons their mass. – Ask a question.
Compared the products of the collisions with the predicted properties of the Higgs boson. – Decide whether the evidence supports the hypothesis.

   b. C, A, D, B

2. a. Easier to communicate quickly in 21st century.

b.

Statement	Advantage, disadvantage, or both?
In an international team, scientists may speak different languages.	both
In an international team, costs can be shared.	advantage
Scientists from different countries may be experts in different things.	advantage
In an international team, scientists may not meet their colleagues often.	disadvantage

7.5 Proton and nucleon numbers

1. Proton number is the number of protons in an atom.
   Mass number is the total number of protons and neutrons in an atom.
   Nucleon number is the total number of protons and neutrons in an atom.

2.

75	23	53	14	8	7	53	16	9	92	7
Re	V	I	Si	O	N	I	S	F	U	N

   Revision is fun.

3.

Atom of the element...	Proton number	Number of neutrons	Nucleon number
hydrogen	1	0	1
helium	2	2	4
beryllium	4	5	9
nitrogen	7	7	14
sodium	11	12	23
sulfur	16	16	32
titanium	22	26	48

4. **a.** 3
   b. 4
   c. Silicon.

d. Gallium.

e. Half.

f. Neon.

8.1 Pure substances

1. One type, elements and compounds, nothing mixed with it, is.

2. **a.** Sample **A** is a pure substance because its temperature does not change while it freezes.
   b. 60 °C

8.2 Drinking seawater

1. Salt – solute;
   seawater – solution;
   water – solvent.

2. Pure, seawater, seawater, evaporates, condenses.

3.
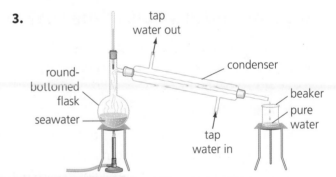

8.3 Chromatography

1. B, D, F, A, C, E

2. **a.** B.
   b. Because the ink spots are at the same heights as the sample from pen B.

Answers

3. **a.** For example – in the production of some COVID-19 vaccines; to test clothes and luggage for explosives; to identify food nutrients.

8.4 Solutions and concentration

1. True – **a**, **b**, **c**.
   False – **d**, **e**, **f**.
   Corrected versions of false statements:
   d. To make a solution more concentrated, add more solute;
   e. To make a solution more dilute, add more solvent;
   f. The more solute particles in 100 cm³ of solution, the more concentrated the solution

2. Beaker B.

3. Diagram the same as B, but with more black particles.

8.5 How much salt is in the sea?

1. **a.** Mass of empty beaker – 120 g; mass of beaker + rock salt – 125.8 g; mass of rock salt (125.8 – 120) = 5.8 g.

   b. A, E, C, B, D, F

   c. Hot apparatus – reduce chance of injury and damage by burning off Bunsen when water has evaporated, wait for the equipment to cool before touching, stand back while heating; salt spitting – burns to skin and damage to eyes; wear eye protection.

   d. Sample may contain less salt; some salt may have left the evaporating basin during the heating stage.

8.6 Chlorine and water

1. Larger samples make the results more reliable and reduce errors.

2. To compare the effect of fluoridation with no fluoridation.

3. 2007–2012 is a longer time frame so they could determine the effects of fluoridation over a longer time period.

4. In towns where the water was fluoridated, the number of 5–6 year olds with missing teeth (from decay) and the number of 12–13 year olds with surface decay decreased. However, the same effect on 5–6 year olds was seen in town D, which did not have fluoridated water. There does not appear to be a link between water fluoridation and the change in the number of 12–13 year olds with decayed, missing or filled teeth.

5. If the water did not contain adequate levels of fluorine, it is possible that the effects of the fluorine may have not been as significant as if the correct levels of fluorine were used.

8.7 Solubility

1. **A, C, E**

2.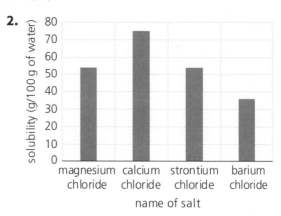

8.8 Investigating temperature and solubility – doing an investigation

1. **a.** Independent – water temperature; dependent – mass of salt; control – water temperature.

   b. i. Measuring cylinder.

   ii. Lab thermometer (the longer one).

   c. 58

d. B. heat the water to the required
temperature; **E.** measure out 100 cm³ of
water and pour into a new beaker;
H. write down the mass of salt added when
some remains undissolved.

8.9 Investigating temperature and solubility – writing up an investigation

1.

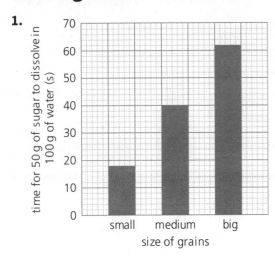

2. a.

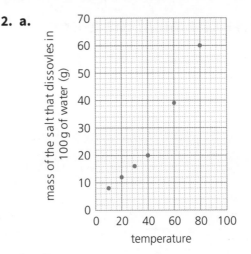

b. D

Extension

Temperature (°C)	Mass of copper sulfate that dissolves in 100 g of water (g)	Mass of sodium carbonate that dissolves in 100 g of water (g)	Mass of potassium chloride that dissolves in 100 g of water (g)

9.1 More chemical reactions

1. In a chemical reaction the atoms rearrange.
In a chemical reaction the atoms join together differently.
In a chemical reaction energy is transferred.
In a chemical reaction the starting substances are reactants.

2. **a.** 2
   b. 2
   c. 4
   d. 4
   e. 16 g

Extension

In one of the reactants, one carbon atom is joined to four hydrogen atoms in a methane molecule. In the other reactant, two chlorine atoms are joined together in a chlorine molecule. In the chemical reaction, the atoms rearrange and join together differently. In one product, a carbon atom is joined to three hydrogen atoms and one chlorine atom. In the other product, one hydrogen atom is joined to one chlorine atom.

9.2 Word equations

1. Reactants – the starting substances in a chemical reaction;
   products – the substances made in a chemical reaction;
   arrow – reacts to make.

2. **a.** Reactants – magnesium and oxygen; product – magnesium oxide.
   b. Reactants – iron and oxygen; product – iron oxide.
   c. Reactants – carbon and oxygen; product – carbon dioxide.
   d. Reactants – sodium hydroxide and hydrochloric acid; products – sodium chloride and water.
   e. Reactants – hydrochloric acid and copper oxide; products – copper chloride and water.

3. **a.** zinc + oxygen → zinc oxide
   b. potassium + oxygen → potassium oxide
   c. carbon + oxygen → carbon dioxide
   d. sulfur + oxygen → sulfur dioxide
   e. silver nitrate + potassium iodide → silver iodide + potassium nitrate
   f. calcium carbonate + sulfuric acid → calcium sulfate + carbon dioxide + water

4. **a.** lithium + oxygen → lithium oxide
   b. calcium + oxygen → calcium oxide
   c. zinc + oxygen → zinc oxide

Extension

a. calcium carbonate → calcium oxide + carbon dioxide
d. aluminium + iodine → aluminium iodide
e. magnesium + sulfuric acid → magnesium sulfate + hydrogen
f. copper oxide + magnesium → magnesium oxide + copper

9.3 Energy changes

1. Exothermic changes include freezing;
   exothermic changes transfer energy to the surroundings;
   exothermic changes include combustion reactions;
   endothermic changes include evaporating;
   endothermic changes transfer energy from the surroundings.

2. Melt, cold, from, start, endothermic.

3. **a.** B (72 – 24) = 48
   D (10 – 23) = –13
   E (86 – 25) = 61
   b. A, B, E
   c. E
   d. C, D
   e. A, B, E

Extension

The water takes energy from the surroundings in order to evaporate.

9.4 Investigating fuels

1. **a.** Volume of water – control; type of fuel – independent; mass of fuel burned – control; temperature change of water – dependent.

   b. i. To reduce error; to make the results more reliable.

   ii. 81 in bottom row.

   iii. $(42 + 38 + 40) \div 3 = 40$

iv. The temperature change of the water is greatest for butanol, so butanol transfers most energy to the water.

Extension

Energy transferred to the air and apparatus.

9.5 Investigating food energy

1. **a.** Thermometer.

   b. Wait for the apparatus to cool before heating, do not touch hot apparatus or water.

   c. i. To reduce (random) error; to make the results more reliable.

ii.

Food	Test number	Water temperature before heating (°C)	Water temperature after heating (°C)	Water temperature change (°C)
nut type 1	1			
	2			
	3			
nut type 2	1			
	2			
	3			
nut type 3	1			
	2			
	3			

   e. Cashew, peanut, walnut.

9.6 Metals and oxygen

1. Oxygen, oxides, iron oxide, reactive.

2. **a.** Lithium, potassium, sodium, magnesium.

   b. Potassium, sodium, lithium, magnesium, gold.

3. **a.** magnesium + oxygen → magnesium oxide

   b. iron + oxygen → iron oxide

   c. potassium + oxygen → potassium oxide

   d. lead + oxygen → lead oxide

   e. tin + oxygen → tin oxide

   f. zinc + oxygen → zinc oxide

Extension

The reaction of magnesium is more vigorous, so it is most reactive. The reaction of copper is least vigorous, so it is least reactive. Zinc and iron are between magnesium and copper, with zinc more reactive than iron.

9.7 Metals and water

1. **a.** Top hazard symbol – corrosive – wear eye protection; place a screen between glass trough and students; do not touch the metal; wear gloves.

Lower hazard symbol – highly flammable – wear eye protection; use a tiny piece of potassium, place a screen between reaction and students; replace the lid on the potassium container as soon as possible.

b. It was easy to cut the potassium; the potassium floated on the surface of the water; the potassium moved around quickly; there was a lilac/purple/mauve flame; the universal indicator solution changed colour from green to purple.

2. True– **a**, **c**.
   False– **b**, **d**.
   Corrected versions of false statements:
   b. Calcium reacts with water to make calcium hydroxide and hydrogen gas.
   d. The word equation for the reaction is sodium + water → sodium hydroxide + hydrogen.

9.8 Metals and acids

1. **a.** Copper, gold.
   b. Magnesium.
   c. Magnesium, zinc, iron, copper/gold.

2. **a.** Hydrochloric – chlorides; nitric – nitrate; sulfuric – sulfates.
   b. i. magnesium + hydrochloric acid → magnesium chloride + hydrogen
   ii. zinc + sulfuric acid → zinc sulfate + hydrogen
   iii. iron + hydrochloric acid → iron chloride + hydrogen
   iv. zinc + hydrochloric acid → zinc chloride + hydrogen

Extension

Hydrochloric acid, magnesium chloride solution, magnesium.

9.9 The reactivity series of metals

1. **a.** Potassium.
   b. Silver/gold.
   c. Two from potassium, sodium, lithium, calcium, magnesium.
   d. Three from lead, copper, silver, gold.

2. **a.** Same concentration of acid each time, same temperature each time.
   b. Zinc.

3. **a.** Copper.
   b. zinc + oxygen → zinc oxide

4. Magnesium – small bubbles on surface of metal; calcium – bubbles vigorously; copper – no reaction.

Extension

Zinc/magnesium more reactive, so they react with oxygen/water instead of the iron.

9.10 Investigating lead in the reactivity series

1. **a.** Magnesium, tin, copper.
   b. i. Zinc – bubbles vigorously with acid, but tin bubbles slowly.
   ii. Tin – bubbles slowly with acid, but lead bubbles very slowly indeed.
   iii. The reactivity of tin is between the reactivity of zinc and lead.
   c. i. Results from the experiment with acid do not show which is more reactive.
   ii. The reaction is likely to take a long time.
   iii. Tin is less reactive than iron, because iron reacts with cold water, but tin does not.

10.1 Proton number and the periodic table

1. True – **a**, **c**.

   False – **b**, **d**.

   Corrected versions of false statements:

   b. In the periodic table, the elements are arranged in order of proton/atomic number;

   d. A helium atom has 2 protons and 2 neutrons, so its proton number is 2.

2. **a.** **i.** 33

   ii. 36

   iii. 47

   b. **i.** Lithium.

   ii. Nitrogen.

   iii. Aluminium.

   iv. Potassium.

   c. **i.** 21

   ii. 17

   iii. 50

   iv. 79

3. Diagram showing 4 small circles in one colour (key – protons) and 5 small circles in another colour (key – neutrons).

10.2 Electrons in atoms

1. Neutrons, protons, 2, 8, chemical.

2.

Element	Number of electrons in one atom	Electron configuration
helium	2	2
lithium	3	2,1
boron	5	2,3
nitrogen	7	2,5
fluorine	9	2,7
magnesium	12	2,8,2

silicon	14	2,8,4
sulfur	16	2,8,6

3. Lithium – 2 electrons in first shell, 1 in second shell; beryllium – 2 in first shell, 2 in second shell; neon – 2 in first shell, 8 in second shell; sodium – 2 in first shell, 8 in second shell, 1 in third shell; magnesium – 2 in first shell, 8 in second shell, 2 in third shell; argon – 2 in first shell, 8 in second shell, 8 in third shell.

10.3 Making ions

1. Ion, electrons, negatively, positively.

2.

Description of ion	Chemical formula of ion
A lithium ion, with a charge of +1	Li^+
A magnesium ion, with a charge of +2	Mg^{2+}
An aluminium ion, with a charge of +3	Al^{3+}
A fluoride ion, with a charge of –1	F^-
A sulfide ion, with a charge of –2	S^{2-}
A nitride ion, with a charge of –3	N^{3-}

3. **A** and **C**.

10.4 Inside ionic compounds

1. Ion – a particle with a positive or negative charge; ionic bonding – electrostatic attraction between positive and negative charges; giant ionic structure – the three-dimensional

pattern of positive and negative charges;
ionic compound – a substance that is made up of positive and negative ions.

2. **A**, **C**, **D**

3. Vrinda.

10.5 Covalent bonding

1. True statements – **a**, **d**, **e**.
   False statements – **b**, **c**, **f**.

Corrected versions of false statements:

b. Each covalent bond holds two atoms together;

c. Compounds of non-metals have covalent bonds;

f. There are three covalent bonds in an ammonia molecule, NH_3.

2. **a.** From top – 4, 1, 8, 2.

   b. Their atoms have a share in the number of electrons needed for a full outer shell (8 for carbon and 2 for hydrogen).

10.6 Covalent structures

1.

Statement	True for substances with simple molecules	True for substances with giant covalent structures	True for simple molecules and giant structures
There are shared pairs of electrons between the atoms.			✓
The atoms are joined by covalent bonds.			✓
There is a three-dimensional network of atoms.		✓	
The molecules are attracted to each other weakly.	✓		
They have low melting points.	✓		
They are in the solid state at room temperature.		✓	
They have high melting points.		✓	
Most are in the gas or liquid state at room temperature.	✓		

2. **a. M**

   b. G

   c. M

   d. M

   e. M

   f. G

3. In a substance with simple molecules, the molecules are attracted to each other only weakly, so little energy is needed to disrupt the structure when the solid melts; but in a substance with a giant covalent structure, atoms are joined together in a three-dimensional structure with strong covalent bonds, so large amounts of energy are needed to break all the covalent bonds when it melts.

10.7 More about structures

1. Electrons, ions, electrons, do not, do, electrostatic, strong, large, high, electrons.

2. Circles with crosses are protons; – symbols are electrons.

3. Copper – metallic;
   sodium chloride – giant ionic;
   hydrogen sulfide – simple molecules;
   silicon dioxide – giant covalent.

4. **A.** metallic; **B.** simple molecules; **C.** giant covalent.

10.8 Life-saving compounds

1. Luther.

2. A, G, D, B, H, E, I, F, C

3. A, C

11.1 Calculating density

1. C, A, D, B

2. **a.** 1 cm × 2 cm × 3 cm = 6 cm^3

   b. 1 cm × 1 cm × 5 cm = 5 cm^3

3. 22 cm^3 – 14 cm^3 = 6 cm^3

4. balsa wood density = 16 g ÷ 8 cm^3 = 2 g/cm^3; oak wood density = 42 g ÷ 6 cm^3 = 7 g/cm^3; copper density = 38 g ÷ 2 cm^3 = 19 g/cm^3; aluminium density = 2.7 g ÷ 1 cm^3 = 2.7 g/cm^3

11.2 Explaining density

1. Density – the mass in a certain volume; mass – the amount of matter in an object; volume – the amount of space an object takes up.

2. Platinum.

3. C

11.3 Using density

1.

Action	Al-Biruni did this	Some or all scientists do this today
Ask scientific questions	✓	✓
Do experiments	✓	✓
Collect data	✓	✓
Make conclusions	✓	✓
Write about their work	✓	✓
Publish their work on the Internet		✓
Specialise in one area of science		✓
Study many areas of science	✓	
Work in international teams		✓

a. Amber, opal, lapis lazuli, diamond, garnet, sapphire.

b. **i.** density = 1.50 g ÷ 1.40 cm^3 = 1.07 g/cm^3

   ii. Amber.

   iii. Test its electrical conductivity; measure how much it changes the direction of light.

11.4 The periodic table: Group 1

1. a. M, O

   b. M, O

   c. O

   d. –

   e. –

   f. –

   g. O

2. a. i.

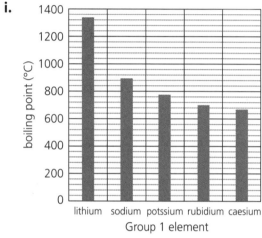

   Group 1 element

   ii. From top to bottom of Group 1, boiling point decreases.

Extension

a. From top to bottom of Group 1, melting point decreases.

b. Group 1 elements have giant metallic structures. From top to bottom of the group, the ions get bigger. This means that electrostatic attractions between positive ions and negative electrons get weaker. As the attractions get weaker, ions leave their fixed positions more easily, so melting point decreases.

11.5 More about Group 1

1. Left column shaded.

2. a. A density = 1.00 g ÷ 1.89 cm³ = 0.529 g/cm³; B density = 3.00 g ÷ 0.14 cm³ = 21.4 g/cm³; C density = 4.00 g ÷ 4.65 cm³ = 0.860 g/cm³; D = 2.00 g ÷ 0.10 cm³ = 20.0 g/cm³

   b. A, C – their densities are much lower than the others.

3. a. i. lithium + water →
            lithium hydroxide + hydrogen

      ii. sodium + water →
            sodium hydroxide + hydrogen

      iii. potassium + water →
            potassium hydroxide + hydrogen

   b. From top to bottom of the group, reactivity increases.

   c. When a Group 1 element reacts with water, each atom gives its outer electron to an atom of another element. From top to bottom of Group 1, the outer electron gets further from the nucleus. The electrostatic attraction between the nucleus and outer electron gets less, so the outer electron is easier to give away. This makes the reactions more and more vigorous from top to bottom.

11.6 The periodic table: Group 2

1. Second from left column shaded.

2. a. Very vigorous bubbles, colourless solution formed.

   b. calcium + water →
            calcium hydroxide + hydrogen

   c. barium + water →
            barium hydroxide + hydrogen

3. a. calcium chloride and hydrogen

   b. calcium + hydrochloric acid →
            calcium chloride + hydrogen

Extension

a. Values correctly plotted on bar chart; x-axis labelled – element; y-axis labelled – hardness (Moh).

b. Hardness decreases down the group; difference in hardness between adjacent elements gets less from top to bottom.

c. Group 2 elements harder than all the Group 1 elements.

12.1 Mass and energy in chemical reactions

1. True – **b, c, f, g**.

   False – **a, d, e**.

   Corrected versions of false statements:

   a. In a chemical reaction, there are the same number of atoms in the products and reactants;

   d. In some chemical reactions, energy is transferred to the surroundings;

   e. In a chemical reaction, the starting substances are called reactants.

2. **a.** 2

   b. 2

   c. 4

   d. 4

   e. There are the same number of atoms of each element in the reactants and in the products.

Extension

a. Sulfur dioxide, oxygen.

b. Sulfur trioxide.

c. Reacts to make.

d. SO_2

e. O_2

f. SO_3

g. 2

h. 100

12.2 Writing symbol equations

1. **a.** O_2

   b. N_2O

   c. 2

   d. 2

   e. 2

2. **a.** $S + O_2 \rightarrow SO_2$

   b. $2Zn + O_2 \rightarrow 2ZnO$

   c. $Mg + 2HCl \rightarrow MgCl_2 + H_2$

   d. $Zn + H_2SO_4 \rightarrow ZnSO_4 + H_2$

   e. $2Na + 2H_2O \rightarrow 2NaOH + H_2$

   f. $2K + 2H_2O \rightarrow 2KOH + H_2$

   g. $Mg + CuO \rightarrow MgO + Cu$

   h. $CuSO_4 + Fe \rightarrow Cu + FeSO_4$

3. **a.** $C + O_2 \rightarrow CO_2$

   b. $2Mg + O_2 \rightarrow 2MgO$

   c. $Zn + 2HCl \rightarrow ZnCl_2 + H_2$

   d. $2Li + 2H_2O \rightarrow 2LiOH + H_2$

   e. $TiCl_4 + 2Mg \rightarrow 2MgCl_2 + Ti$

12.3 Metal displacement reactions

1. Copper, iron sulfate, displacement, more, copper, displaces, more, less.

2.

Metal \ Compound	magnesium chloride solution	iron chloride solution	lead nitrate solution	copper oxide
magnesium		✓	✓	✓
zinc		✓	✓	✓
iron			✓	✓
lead				✓
copper				

Answers

3. **a.** iron + copper sulfate → iron sulfate + copper

   b. magnesium + lead nitrate →
   magnesium nitrate + lead

   c. iron + copper oxide → iron oxide + copper

   d. zinc + iron nitrate → zinc nitrate + iron

   e. zinc + lead oxide → zinc oxide + lead

   f. magnesium + copper chloride →
   magnesium chloride + copper

Extension

a. Iron oxide and aluminium.

b. Bright sparks/flames.

c. aluminium + iron oxide →
aluminium oxide + iron

12.4 Extracting metals

1. More, more, more, more.

2. **a.** Potassium, sodium, lithium, calcium, magnesium.

   b. Zinc, lead, iron, copper.

   c. Silver, gold.

3. Carbon can only displace metals from their compounds if the metal is below carbon in the reactivity series.

4. **a.** tin oxide + carbon → tin + carbon dioxide

   b. lead oxide + carbon → lead + carbon dioxide

Extension

a. Sodium, magnesium.

b. sodium + titanium chloride →
sodium chloride + titanium

magnesium + titanium chloride →
magnesium chloride + titanium

12.5 Extracting copper

1. Environmental impacts – **A, C, D, F**.
   Demand for copper increasing – **B, E**.

2. **a.** Any sensible examples, for example computers, copper cables, copper water pipes.

b. **A, C, B, D**

c. copper sulfate + iron → iron sulfate + copper

3. **a.** Phytomining.

   b. Recycling.

12.6 Making salts from acids and metals

1. Dasbala.

2. Dilute hydrochloric acid, corrosive – wear eye protection and do not touch;
   hydrogen gas, forms explosive mixture with air – keep away from flames;
   hot equipment and solutions, burns – wait for apparatus to cool before touching;
   sharp edges of broken apparatus, cuts and damage to eyes – wear eye protection and inform teacher of breakages.

3. **A, D, F, B, E, C**

Extension

Calcium and sulfuric acid.

12.7 More about salts

1. True – **b, e, f**.
   False – **a, c, d**.
   Corrected versions of false statements:
   a. A salt is a compound made when a metal ion replaces a hydrogen ion in an acid;
   c. Hydrochloric acid makes chloride salts;
   d. Sulfuric acid makes sulfate salts

2. **a.** Zinc chloride.

   b. Magnesium sulfate.

   c. Magnesium chloride.

   d. Iron sulfate.

   e. Magnesium nitrate.

   f. Zinc nitrate.

3. Collect some gas, light a splint, place the lighted splint in the gas, if the splint goes out with a squeaky pop the gas is hydrogen.

4. **a.** magnesium + hydrochloric acid →
        magnesium chloride + hydrogen

   b. zinc oxide + hydrochloric acid →
        zinc chloride + water

   c. copper carbonate + nitric acid →
        copper nitrate + carbon dioxide + water

   d. nickel oxide + sulfuric acid →
        nickel sulfate + water

   e. magnesium + sulfuric acid →
        magnesium sulfate + hydrogen

12.8 Making salts from acids and carbonates

1.

	copper carbonate	magnesium carbonate	zinc carbonate
hydrochloric acid	copper chloride	magnesium chloride	zinc chloride
nitric acid	copper nitrate	magnesium nitrate	zinc nitrate
sulfuric acid	copper sulfate	magnesium sulfate	zinc sulfate

2. **a.** Copper chloride.

   b. Carbon dioxide.

3. **a.** copper carbonate + hydrochloric acid →
        copper chloride + carbon dioxide + water

   b. zinc carbonate + sulfuric acid →
        zinc sulfate + carbon dioxide + water

   c. magnesium carbonate + nitric acid →
        magnesium nitrate + carbon dioxide + water

   d. copper carbonate + sulfuric acid →
        copper sulfate + carbon dioxide + water

4. **a.** Stops bubbling.

   b. B, E, F

   c. E, F

Extension

Solution heats more evenly.

12.9 Rates of reaction

1. **a.** For example, rusting.

   b. For example, making medicines.

2. **a.** calcium carbonate + hydrochloric acid →
        calcium chloride + carbon dioxide + water

   b. The gas made in the reaction is soluble in water.

   c. i. D

   ii. E

   iii. D

   iv. D

   v. E

   vi. E

   d. From top – **iii** and **vi**; **ii** and **iv**; **i** and **v**.

12.10 Concentration and reaction rate

1. **a. i.** Flavia.

   ii. Harry.

   iii. Rebecca.

   b. Concentration of acid – independent; volume of acid – control; type of acid – control; time for zinc to finish reacting – dependent; size of zinc pieces – control; mass of zinc – control.

2. Diagram on right.

3. Collide, more, collide, faster.

Extension

Diagram and label showing that, if there are more acid particles in the solution, they will collide more frequently with the zinc.

12.11 Temperature and reaction rate

1. **a. i.** Ebba.

   ii. Wanda.

   b. i. Dependent and independent variables are continuous.

   ii. Graph correctly plotted, with axes labelled as stated.

iii. The value at 60 °C; solutions had cooled down.

iv. Increase reliability / accuracy

12.12 Surface area and reaction rate

1. A

2. a. One of the products, carbon dioxide, escapes as a gas as it is made.

b. i.

Size of pieces	Time for mass to decrease by 0.8 g (seconds)
big	140
medium	93
small / powder	30

ii.

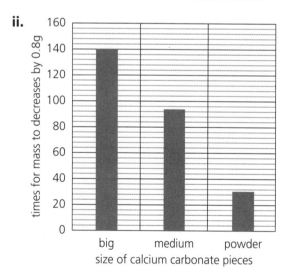

size of calcium carbonate pieces

iii. As the size of pieces decreases, the rate of reaction increases. This is because – for a given mass of substance – the smaller the pieces, the greater the surface area and the greater the number of particles that are exposed for collision with acid particles in the solution.

13.1 Continental drift

1. True – **a, c, d.**
False statements – **b, e, f.**
Corrected versions of false statements:
   b. There are about 12 tectonic plates.
   e. There are convection currents in the mantle.
   f. The moving of tectonic plates is called continental drift.

2. a. Towards.

   b. Any two where the arrows are pointing in opposite directions, for example: Nazca and Pacific; South American and African; African and Antarctic.

   c. The South American and African plates are moving apart.

   d. Any three sensible questions that can be answered by looking at the map.

13.2 Evidence from fossils

1. a. *Glossopteris.*

   b. South America and Africa.

   c. For example, Antarctica, since it is close to the other two continents on which *Mesosaurus* fossils have been found.

2. Similar rock types / strata on neighbouring continents; shape of South America and Africa look as though they could fit together.

13.3 Evidence from seafloor spreading

1. Tectonic plate – the approximately 12 slabs of solid rock that make up the Earth's crust and uppermost mantle;
continental drift – the movement of tectonic plates over millions of years;
seafloor spreading – the movement of the seafloor away from the two sides of an oceanic ridge;
oceanic ridge – a mountain chain on the seafloor;
earthquake – a sudden violent shaking of the ground;
volcano – an opening in the Earth's crust that liquid rock and other materials escape from.

2. C, E, A, D, B

3. D

Glossary

Accurate Accurate data is data that is close to the true value.

Acidic A solution is acidic if its pH is less than 7.

Acidity A chemical property that describes how acidic a substance is.

Alkaline A solution is alkaline if its pH is greater than 7.

Analogy A comparison between one thing and another that helps to explain something. It can be used as a model.

Atom The smallest part of an element that can exist.

Balancing number The balancing numbers in a chemical equation show the ratio of the numbers of particles of the reactants and products. A balancing number is written to the left of its chemical formula.

Boiling The change of state from liquid to gas that only happens if the liquid is hot enough.

Boiling point The temperature at which a substance boils.

Brittle A material is brittle if it breaks easily when hit.

Chemical formula The chemical formula of a substance gives the relative number of atoms of each element in the substance.

Chemical reaction A change in which atoms are rearranged and join together differently to make new substances.

Chemical symbol The internationally recognised one- or two-letter code for an element.

Chromatography A method to separate and identify the substances in a mixture. It works if all the substances in a mixture dissolve in the same solvent.

Compound A substance made up of atoms of two or more substances, strongly joined together.

Compress Make smaller by pressing.

Concentrated A solution containing a large amount of solute dissolved in a solvent.

Concentration The amount of solute that is dissolved in a certain volume of solution or solvent.

Conductor A substance that allows heat and/or electricity to pass through it easily.

Crust The outer layer of the Earth, made of solid rock.

Density The mass of a material in a certain volume. It is calculated using the formula $density = \dfrac{mass}{volume}$.

Ductile A material is ductile if it can be pulled into wires.

Electron A tiny sub-atomic particle with a negative charge that moves around in an atom, outside the nucleus. It has a single negative charge.

Its relative mass is $\dfrac{1}{2000}$.

Element A substance that is made of one type of atom that cannot be split into other substances.

Flammable If a material burns easily, it is flammable.

Giant covalent structure A three-dimensional network of atoms that are joined together by covalent bonds.

Giant ionic structure The three-dimensional structure of positive and negative ions in an ionic compound.

Giant metallic structure A three-dimensional pattern of positive metal ions held together by moving electrons.

Hazard A possible source of danger.

Hazard symbol A warning symbol on a substance that shows what harm it might cause if not handled properly.

Indicator A solution of a dye that turns a different colour in acidic and alkaline solutions.

Inert A substance is inert if it does not take part in chemical reactions.

Inner core The solid iron and nickel at the centre of the Earth.

Lava Liquid rock that is on, or above, the surface of the Earth.

Malleable A material is malleable if it can be hammered into shape without cracking.

Mantle The layer of the Earth beneath the crust. It is solid but can flow slowly. It goes down almost halfway to the centre of the Earth.

Melting The change of state from solid to liquid.

Melting point The temperature at which a substance changes from the solid to the liquid state.

Metal An element on the left of the stepped line of the periodic table. Most metals are good conductors of heat and electricity.

Metal displacement reaction In a metal displacement reaction, a more reactive metal displaces (pushes out) a less reactive metal from its compound.

Mineral salts/minerals Dissolved compounds needed by plant and animal cells to grow and remain healthy.

Model A way of representing something that you cannot see or experience directly. A model may be a physical model built on a different scale to the original system, or it may take the form of equations.

Molecule A particle made up of two or more atoms, strongly joined together.

Neutral (1) A solution is neutral if its pH is 7 – for example, pure water is neutral. (2) A particle is neutral if it is neither positively nor negatively charged, for example an atom of an element or a neutron in the nucleus of an atom.

Neutron A tiny sub-atomic particle with no charge that is found in the nucleus of an atom. The relative mass of a neutron is 1.

Non-metal An element on the right of the stepped line of the periodic table. Most non-metals do not conduct heat or electricity.

Glossary

Nucleon number The total number of protons and neutrons in an atom.

Nucleons Protons and neutrons.

Nucleus The central part of an atom, made up of protons and neutrons.

Ore A rock that a metal can be extracted from.

Particles The tiny pieces of matter that everything is made from.

Peer review The checking of scientific research by other experts.

Products The substances that are made in a chemical reaction.

Properties The properties of a substance describe what it is like and what it does.

Proton A tiny sub-atomic particle with a positive charge that is found in the nucleus of an atom. The relative mass of a proton is 1.

Proton number The number of protons in an atom of an element. Also called the atomic number.

Pure substance A substance that consists of one substance only. It is not mixed with anything, and all its particles are identical.

Rate of a reaction The rate of a chemical reaction is the amount of reactant used up, or the amount of product made, in a given time.

Reactants The starting substances in a chemical reaction.

Reactivity series A list of metals in order of how readily they react with other substances, such as water, oxygen, and dilute acids.

Reactivity The tendency of a substance to take part in a chemical reaction.

Reliable You can obtain reliable data by making enough measurements.

Risk The chance of injury from a hazard. A combination of the probability that something will happen and the consequence if it did.

Salt A compound made when a metal ion replaces the hydrogen ion in an acid.

Scientific question A question that can be answered using evidence or data.

Secondary data Evidence or data that has been collected by someone else.

Solubility The maximum mass of solute that can dissolve in 100 g of solvent.

Sonorous Metals are sonorous – they make a ringing sound when hit.

States of matter Most substances can exist as a solid, liquid, or gas. These are the states of matter.

Steels Alloys of iron.

Strong A material is strong if a large force is needed to break it.

Sub-atomic particles The particles that make up an atom, including protons and neutrons in the nucleus, and electrons outside the nucleus.

Substance A material that has one type of matter.

Symbol equation A symbol equation uses chemical formulae to represent a chemical reaction. It shows the relative number of particles of each of the reactants and products.

Universal indicator A mixture of dyes that changes colour to show how acidic or alkaline a solution is.

Vitamins Substances needed in tiny amounts in the diet to help chemical reactions take place in cells.

Word equation A word equation summarises a chemical reaction in words. It shows the reactants and products. The arrow means 'react to make'.